Mandalas

Coloring Book

For adults

Vol. 2

James S. Johnson

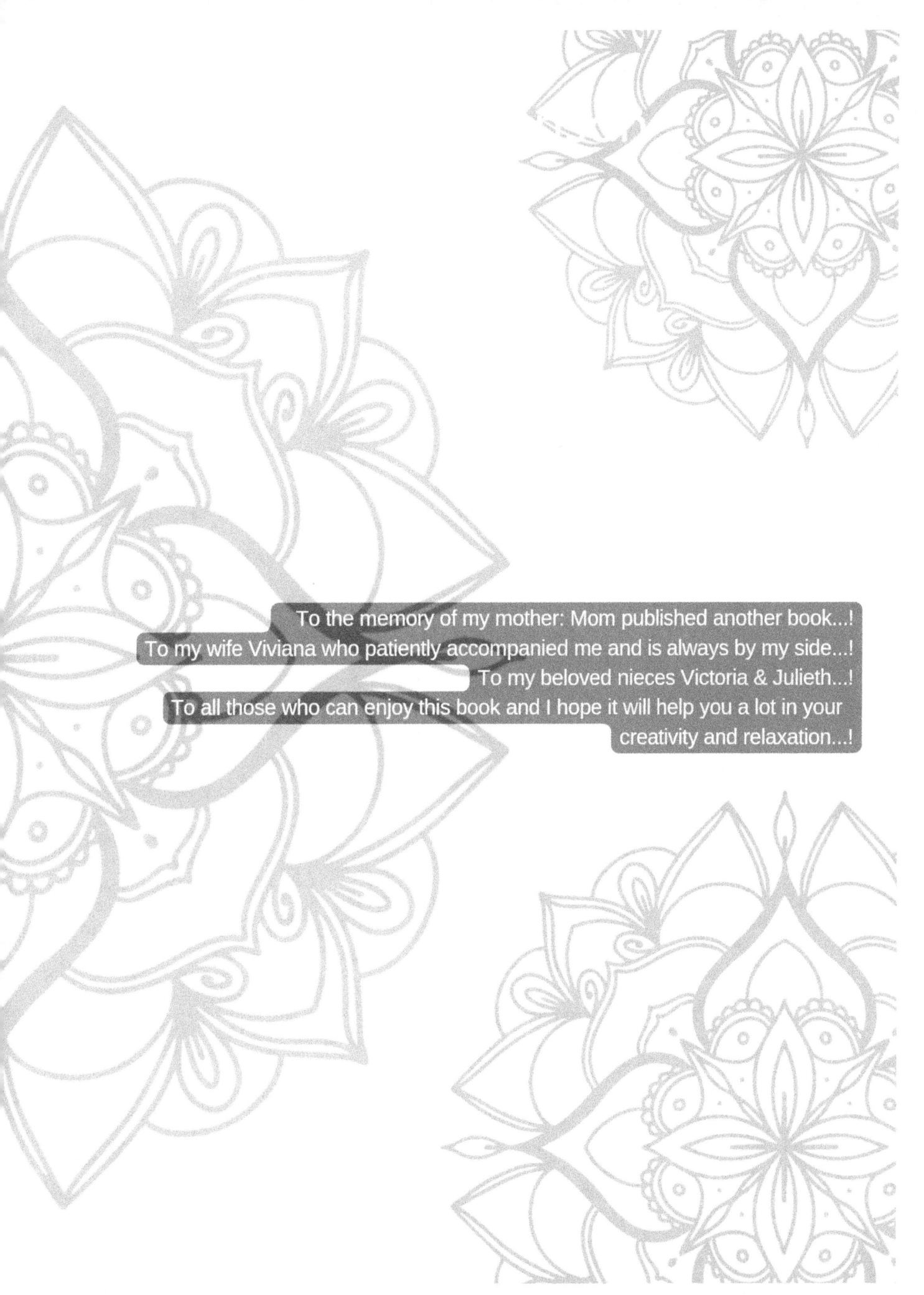

To the memory of my mother: Mom published another book...!
To my wife Viviana who patiently accompanied me and is always by my side...!
To my beloved nieces Victoria & Julieth...!
To all those who can enjoy this book and I hope it will help you a lot in your creativity and relaxation...!

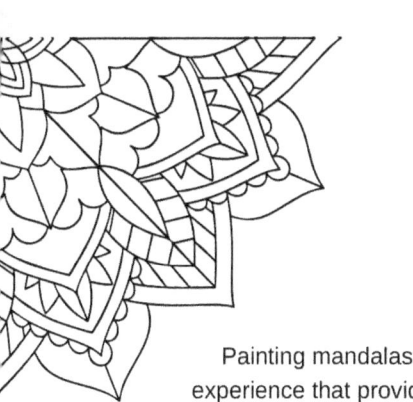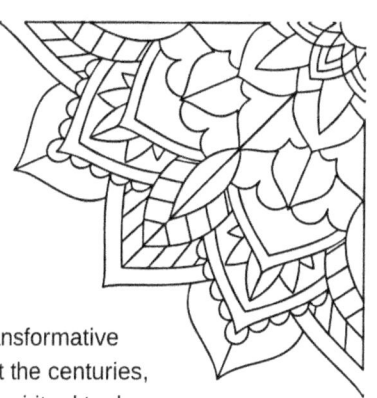

Painting mandalas is an activity that goes beyond simply coloring images. It is a transformative experience that provides a series of benefits for the mind, body, and spirit. Throughout the centuries, mandalas have been used in different cultures and traditions as sacred symbols and spiritual tools. Nowadays, the act of painting mandalas has become a popular practice in art therapy and self-exploration.

What exactly is a mandala? The word "mandala" comes from Sanskrit and means "circle" or "center." A mandala is a symbolic and artistic representation of the wholeness of the universe. It consists of a circular design composed of repeating geometric shapes and patterns in a balanced and harmonious structure. Mandalas capture the essence of the beauty and complexity of life itself.

One of the primary advantages of painting mandalas is its ability to induce a state of relaxation and reduce stress. As you immerse yourself in the task of coloring, you detach from everyday concerns and focus on the present moment. The concentration required to select colors and complete the details of the mandala creates a kind of active meditation, allowing your mind to quiet down and find calm.

In addition to relaxation, painting mandalas also stimulates creativity. As you choose colors and apply different coloring techniques, you exercise your imagination and unleash your artistic side. There are no fixed rules in painting mandalas, giving you the freedom to explore and experiment with different color combinations and styles. Each mandala you create becomes a unique expression of your own creativity.

Mandala therapy has been widely used in the fields of psychology and art therapy. Painting mandalas can be a powerful tool for processing emotions and unlocking the subconscious. By immersing yourself in the activity, you can access parts of yourself that may be hidden or repressed, allowing for greater understanding and emotional healing. Mandalas act as a mirror of your inner world, revealing patterns and symbols that can offer valuable insights into your own life and experiences.

Another benefit of painting mandalas is that it connects you with the spiritual aspect of your being. Mandalas have been used for centuries as sacred symbols in various spiritual traditions. Their circular shape represents the wholeness and unity of all things. By engaging with mandalas, you can experience a sense of transcendence and connection with something greater than yourself. Painting mandalas can be a deeply spiritual experience, allowing you to explore your own essence and find a deeper sense of purpose in your life.

In summary, painting mandalas is a therapeutic and meaningful activity that offers a wide range of benefits for those who embark on it. These benefits encompass both mental and physical well-being and can have a lasting impact on your daily life. By immersing yourself in the colors and patterns of mandalas, you embark on a journey of self-discovery, relaxation, and creativity. You will experience a sense of calm, balance, and connection with your inner self. Whether you are a beginner or an experienced artist, painting mandalas is an accessible and rewarding activity for all. Embark on this therapeutic adventure and let the mandalas guide you toward greater harmony and well-being.

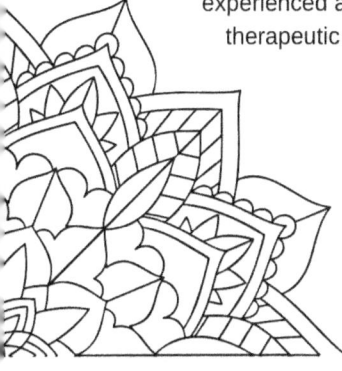

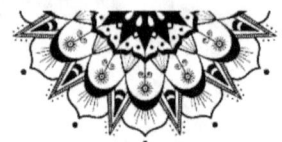

"The only way to do great work is to love what you do." - Steve Jobs

Notes

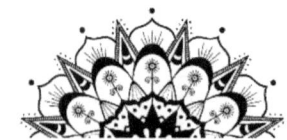

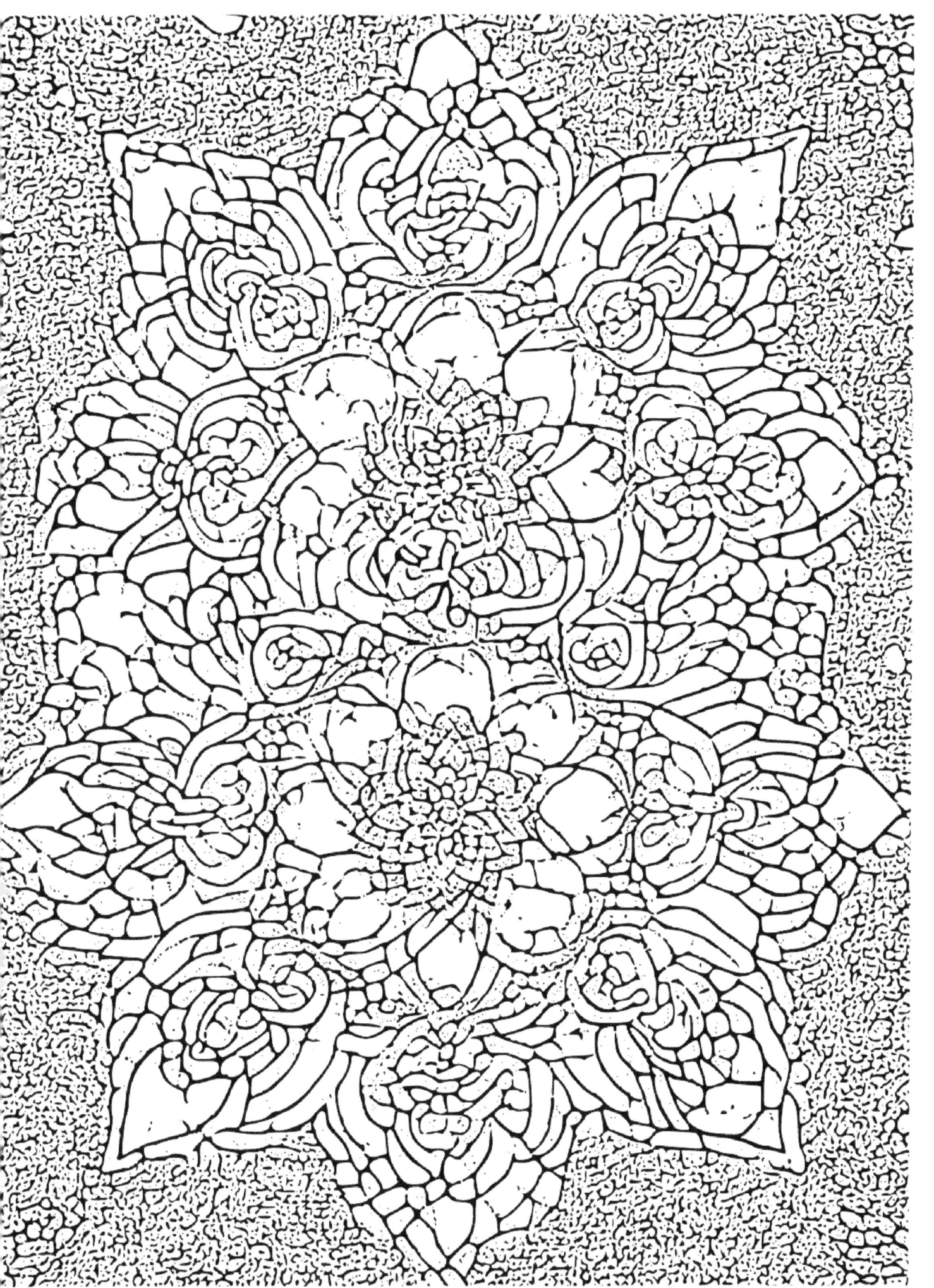

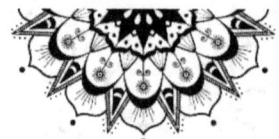

"In the middle of every difficulty lies opportunity." - Albert Einstein

Notes

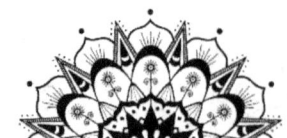

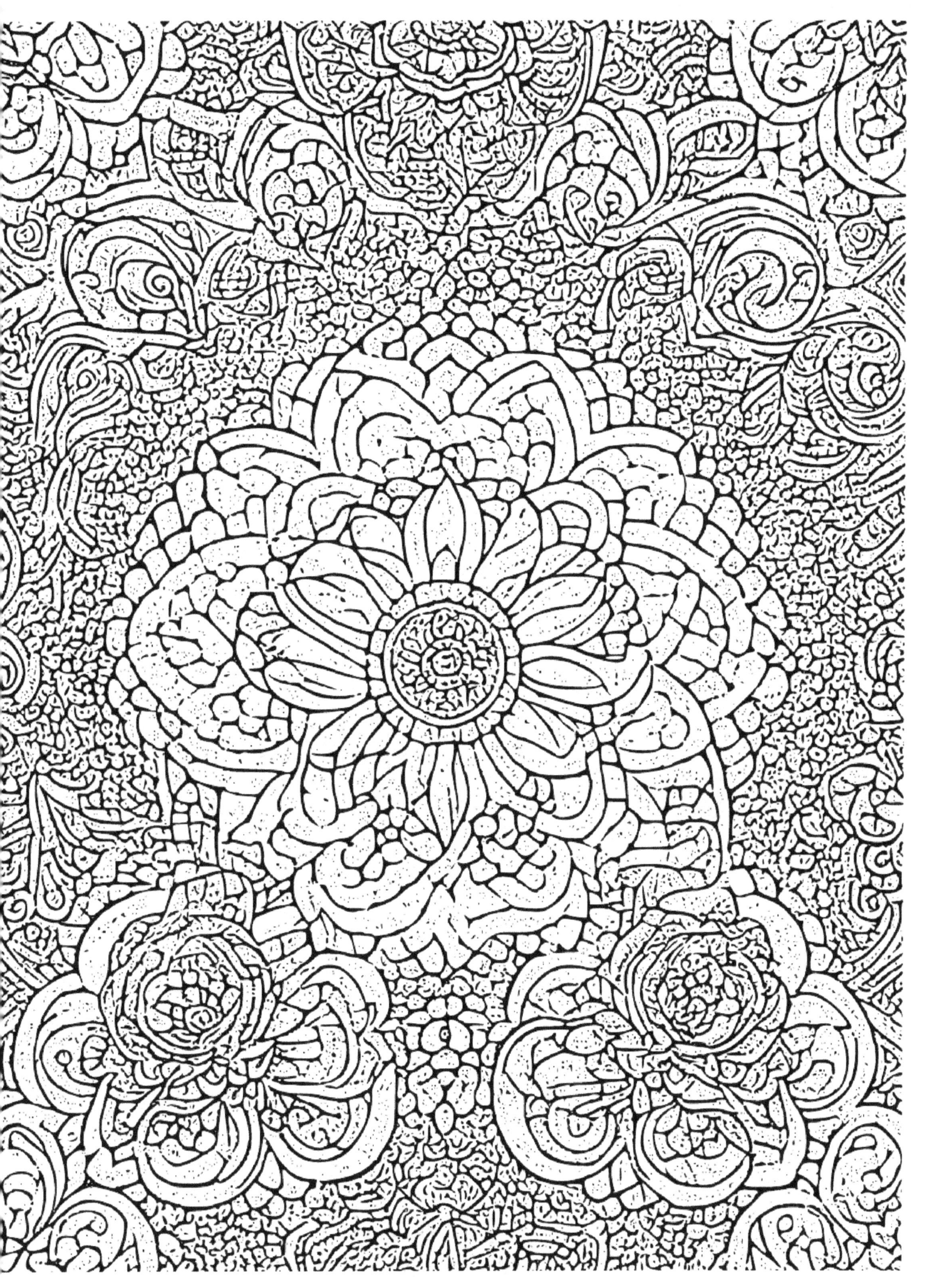

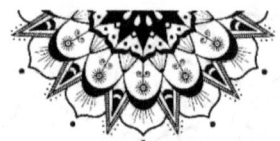

"The true sign of intelligence is not knowledge but imagination." - Albert Einstein

Notes

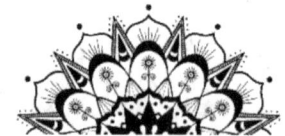

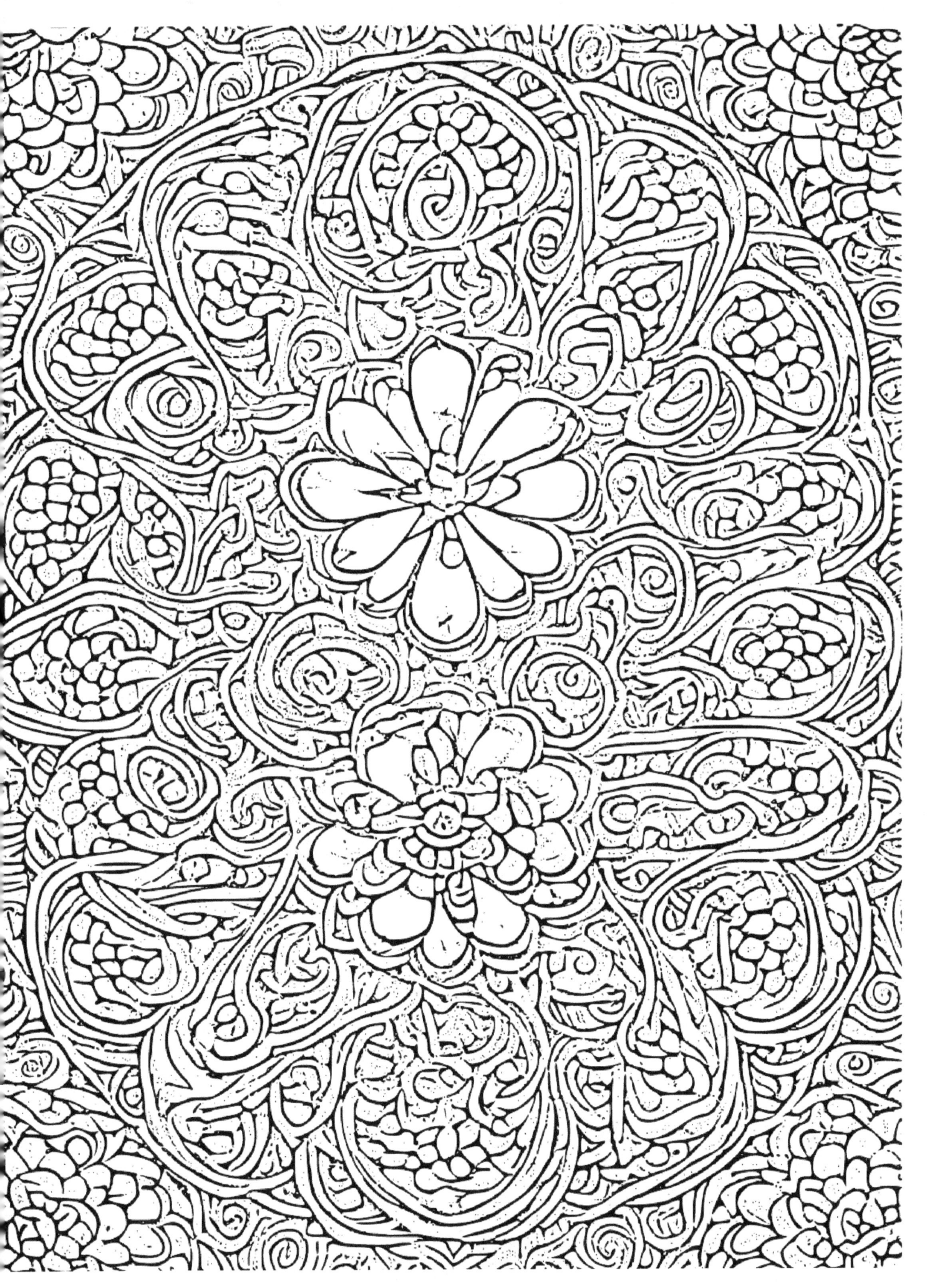

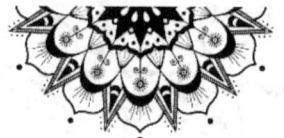

"Believe you can and you're halfway there." - Theodore Roosevelt

Notes

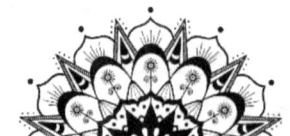

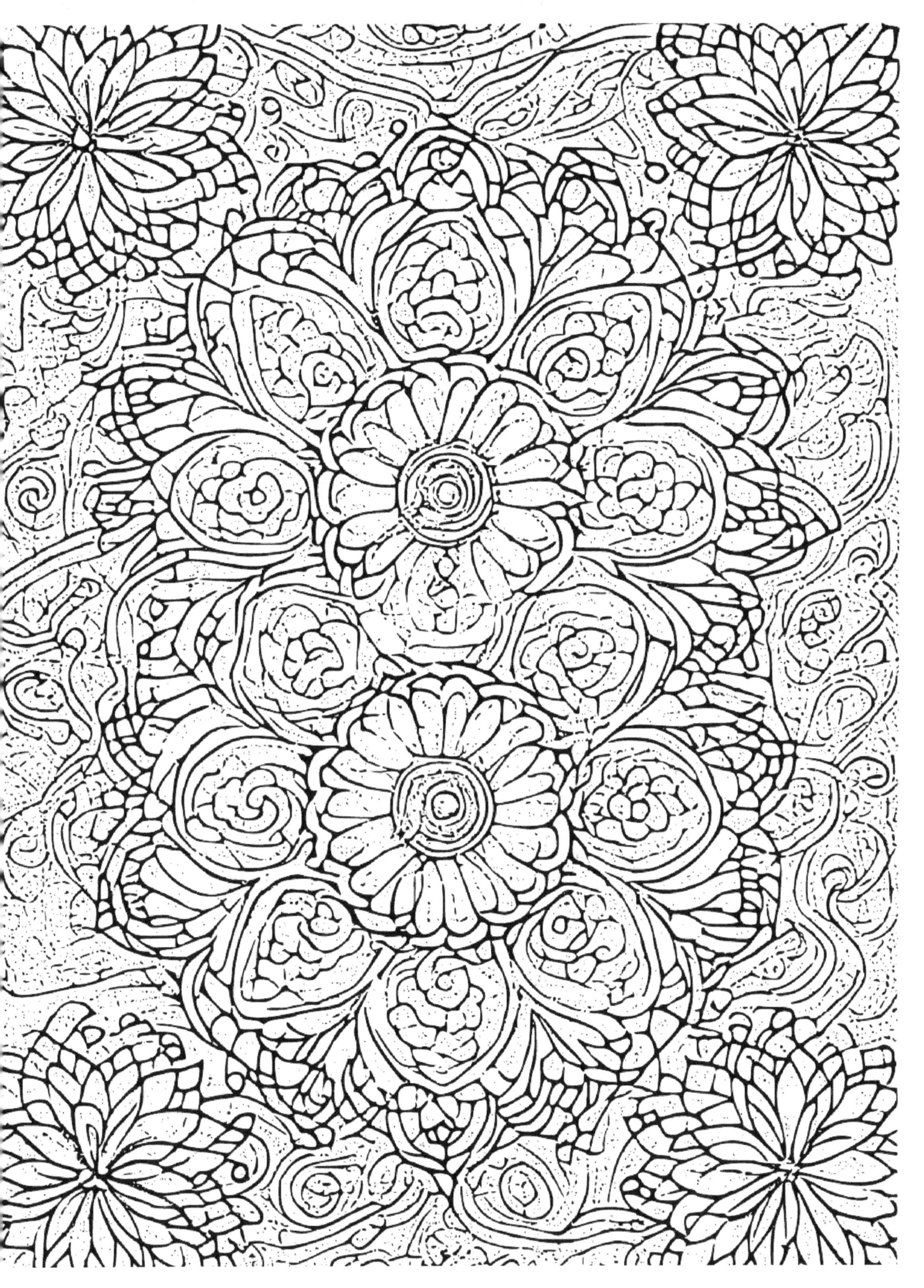

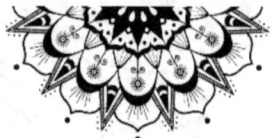

"The only limit to our realization of tomorrow will be our doubts of today." - Franklin D. Roosevelt

Notes

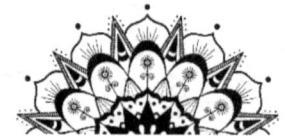

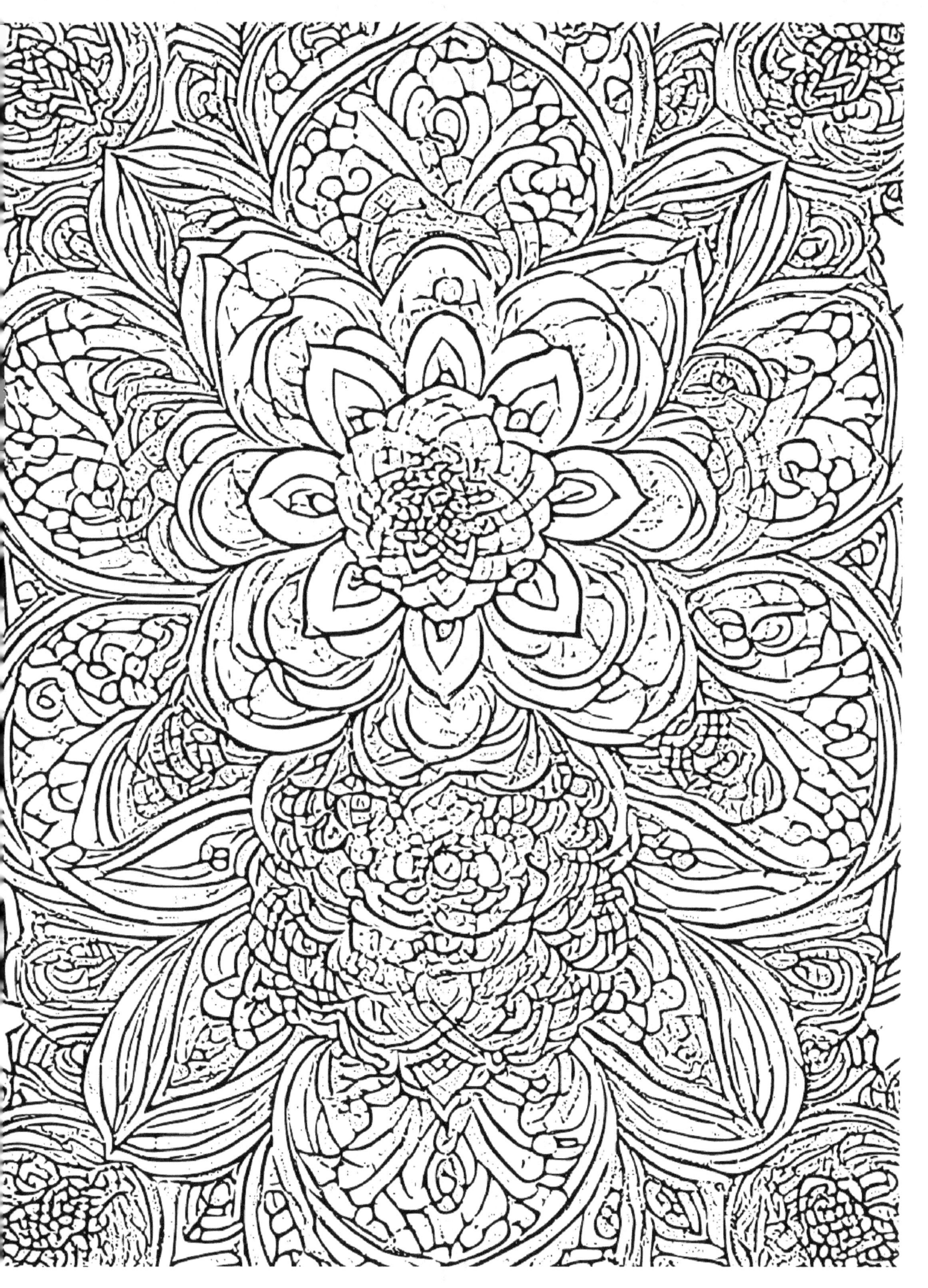

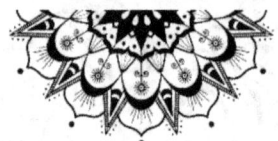

"Success is not the key to happiness. Happiness is the key to success. If you love what you are doing, you will be successful." - Albert Schweitzer

Notes

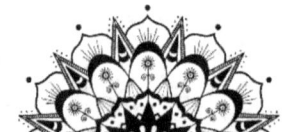

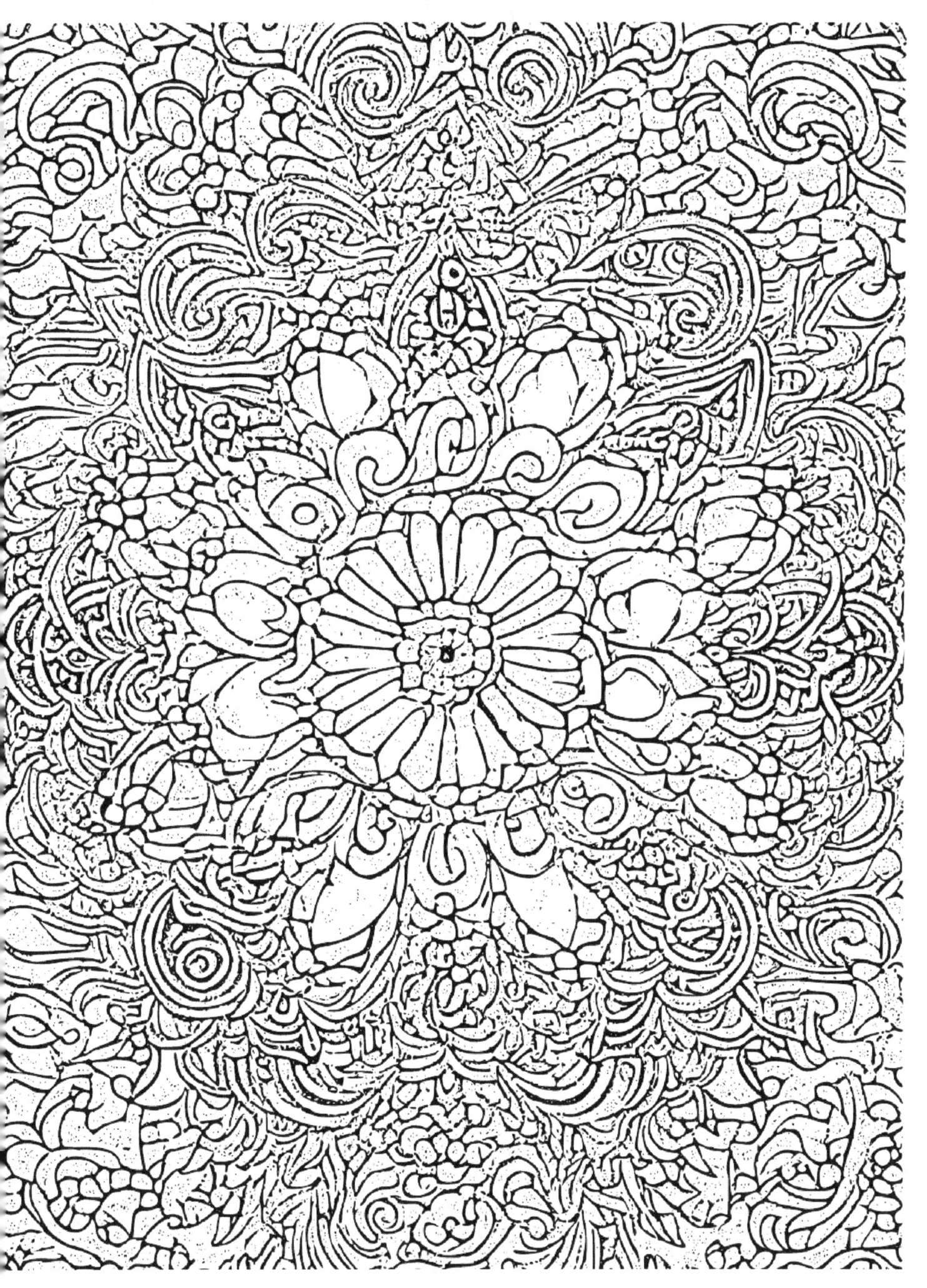

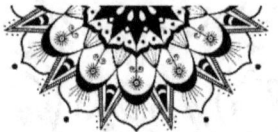

"The best way to predict the future is to create it." - Peter Drucker

Notes

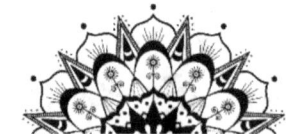

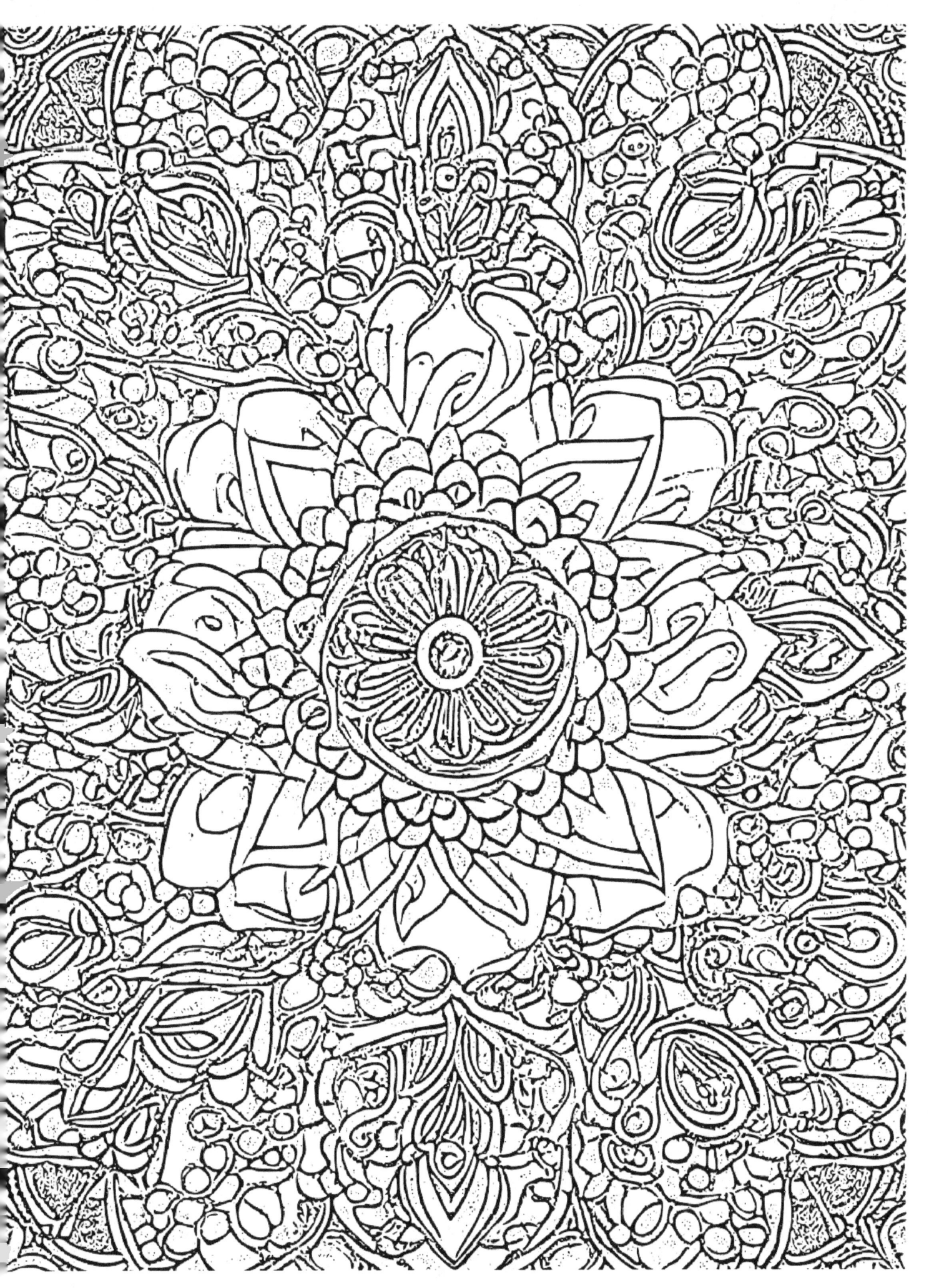

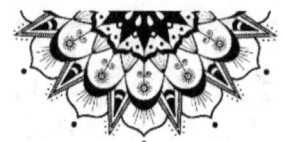

"The only person you are destined to become is the person you decide to be." - Ralph Waldo Emerson

Notes

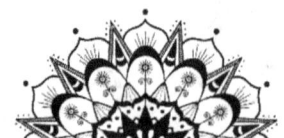

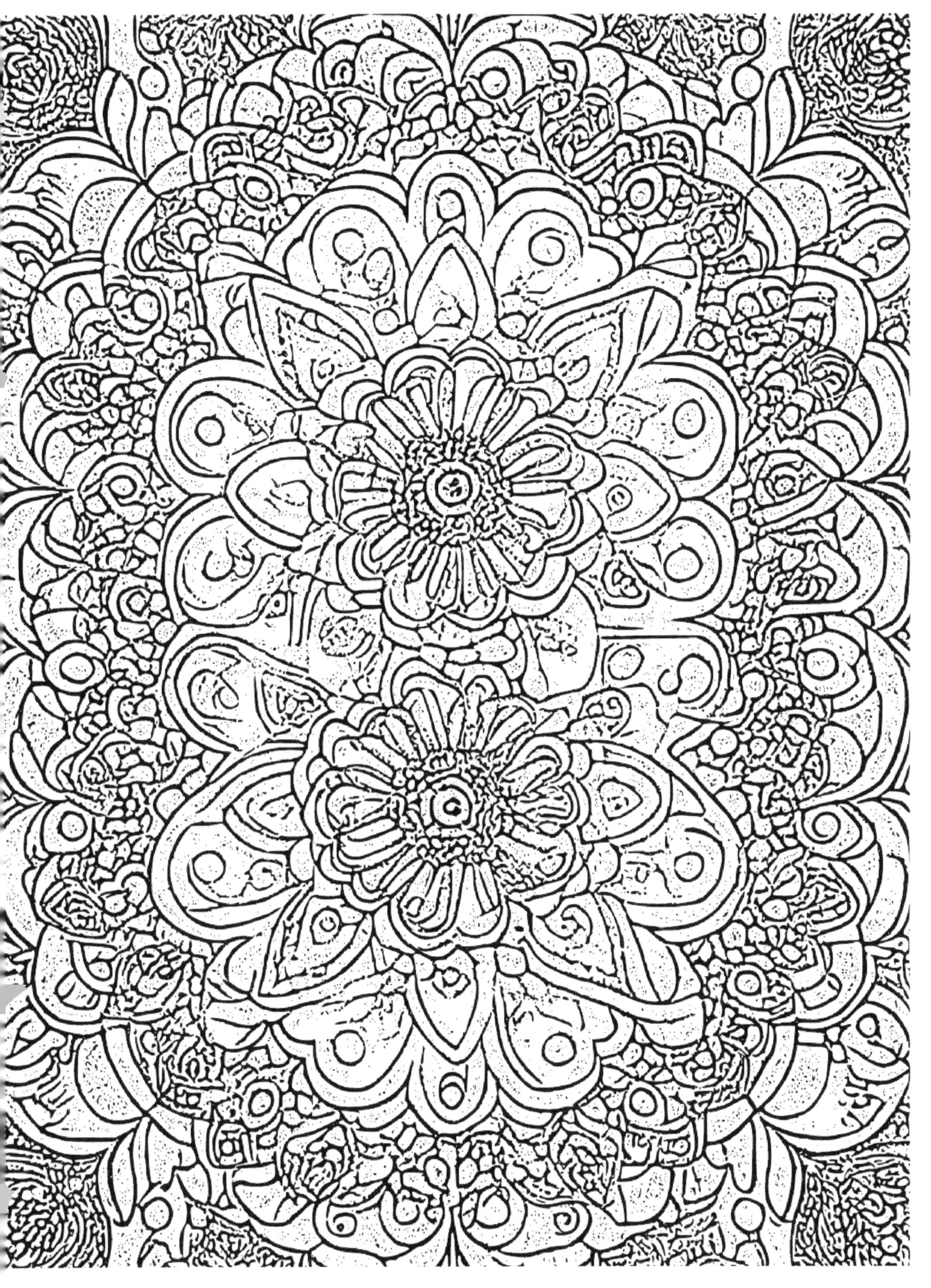

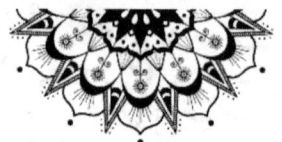

"I have not failed. I've just found 10,000 ways that won't work." – Thomas Edison

Notes

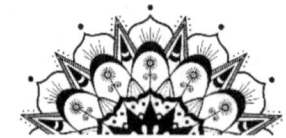

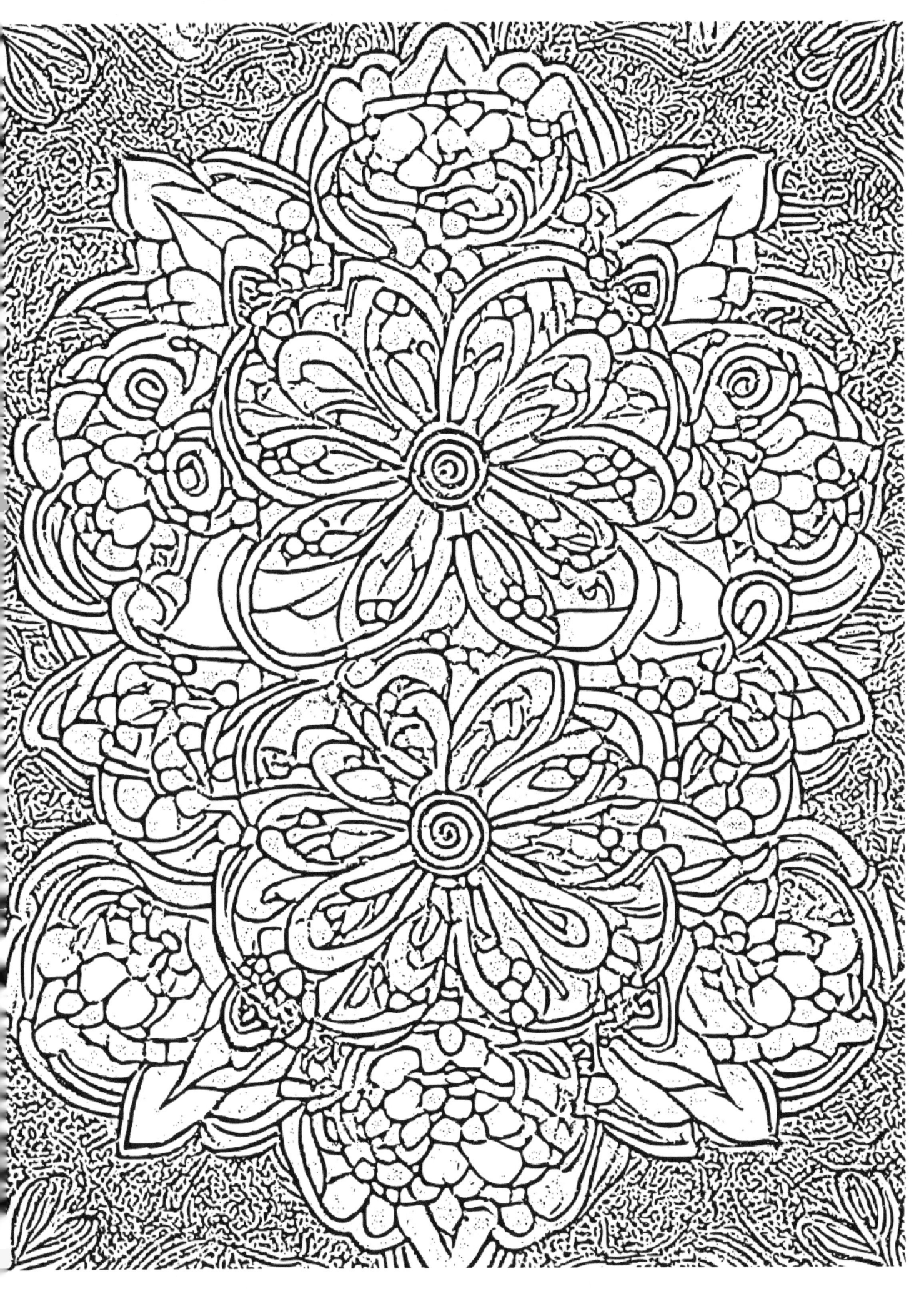

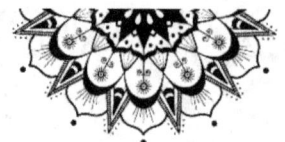

"Don't watch the clock; do what it does. Keep going." - Sam Levenson

Notes

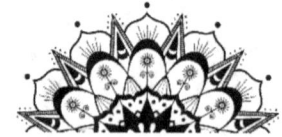

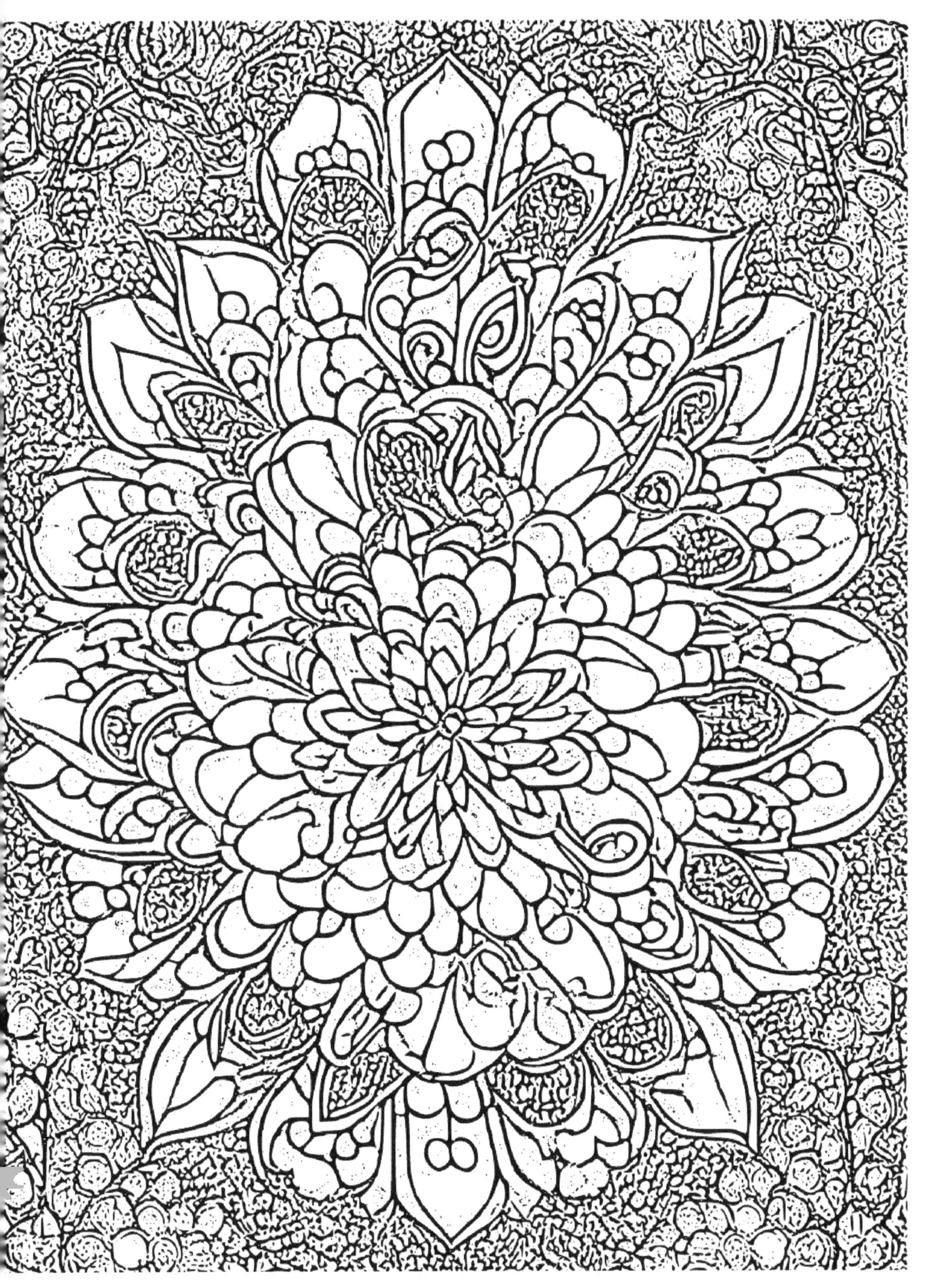

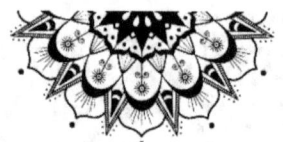

"The greatest glory in living lies not in never falling, but in rising every time we fall." - Nelson Mandela

Notes

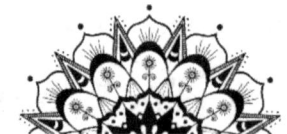

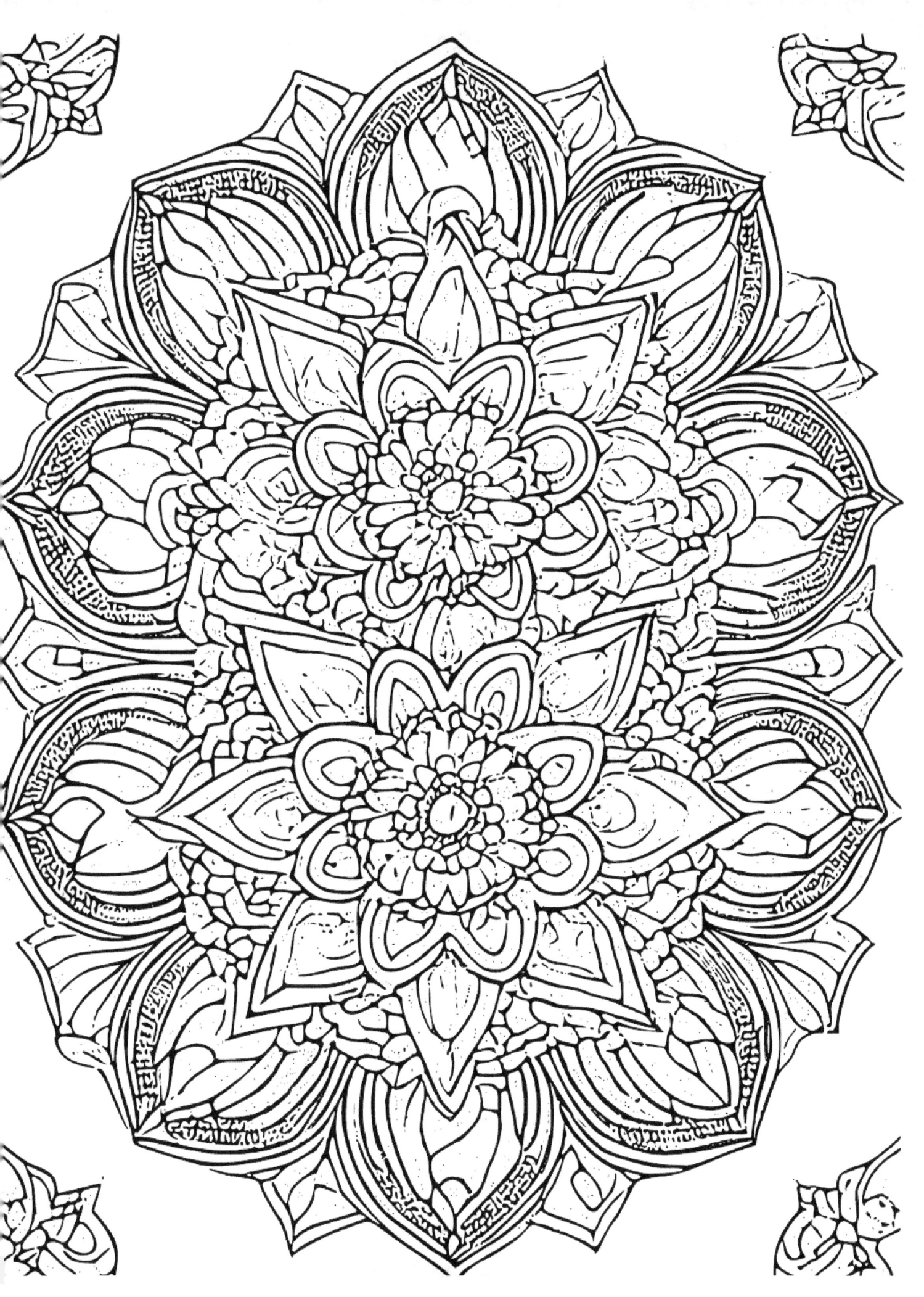

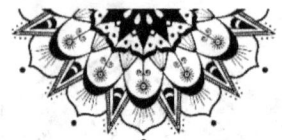

"Your time is limited, don't waste it living someone else's life." - Steve Jobs

Notes

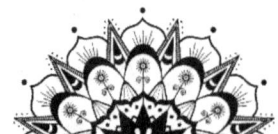

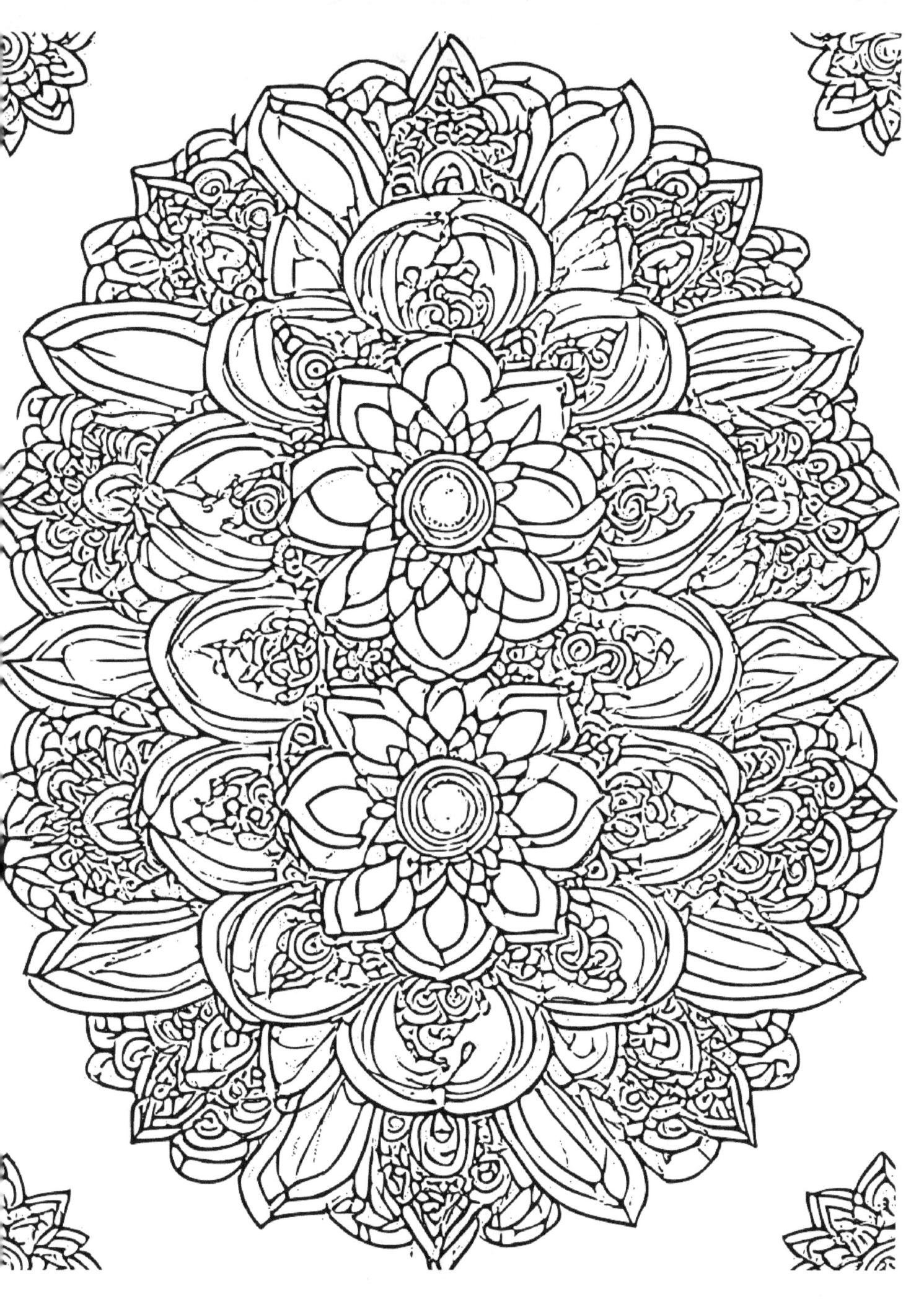

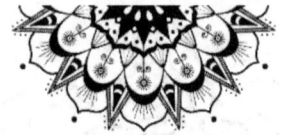

"The present is theirs; the future, for which I really worked, is mine." - Nikola Tesla

Notes

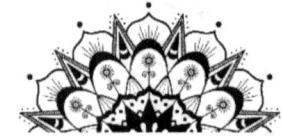

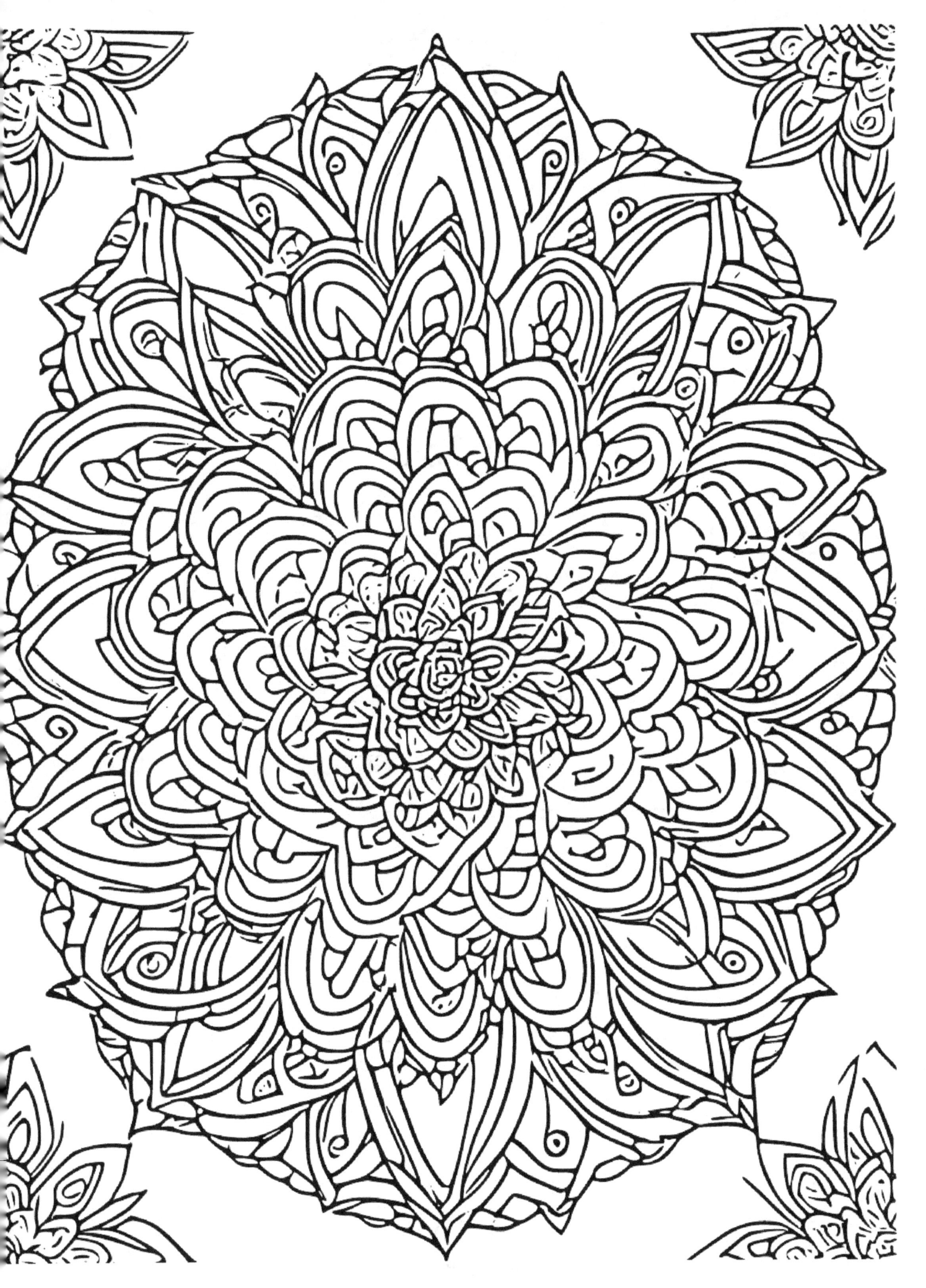

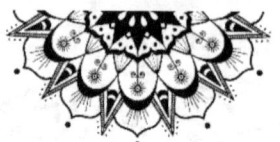

"Success is not final, failure is not fatal: It is the courage to continue that counts." - Winston Churchill

Notes

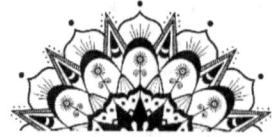

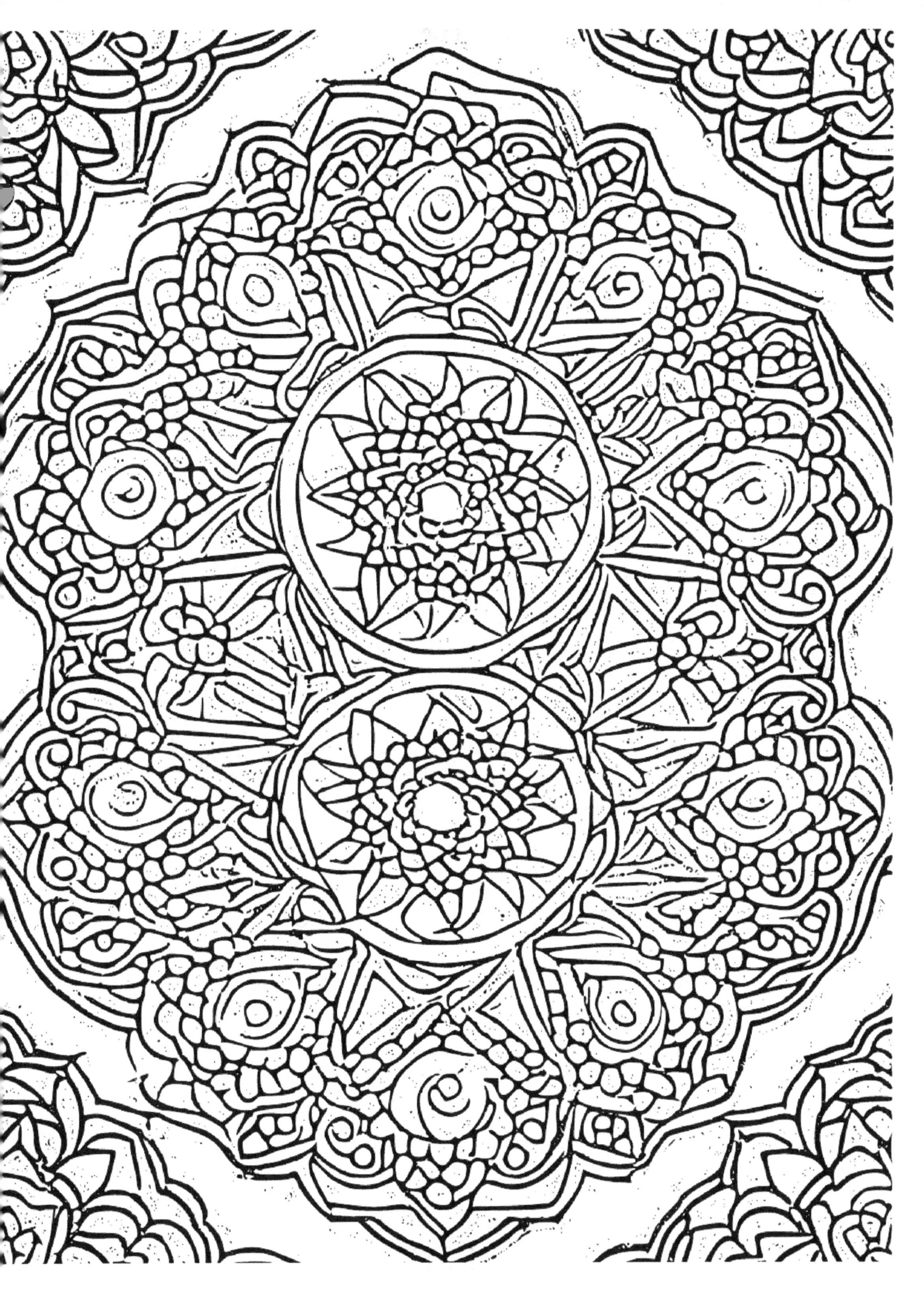

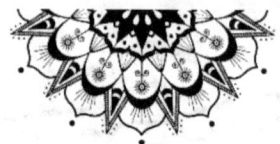

"The future belongs to those who believe in the beauty of their dreams." - Eleanor Roosevelt

Notes

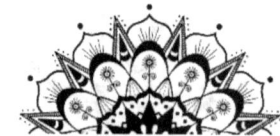

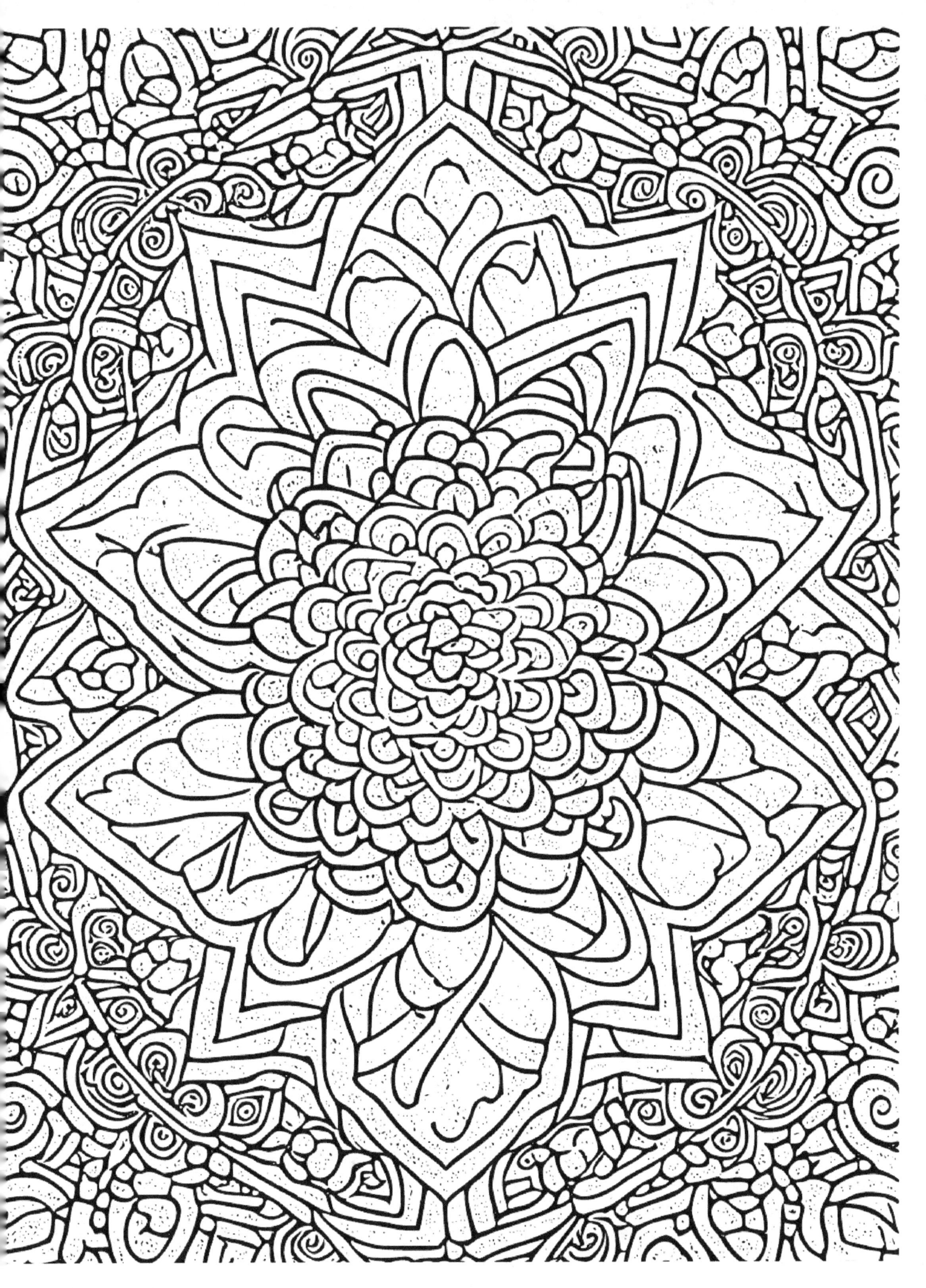

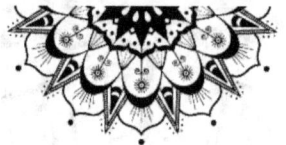

"You miss 100% of the shots you don't take." - Wayne Gretzky

Notes

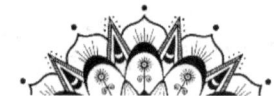

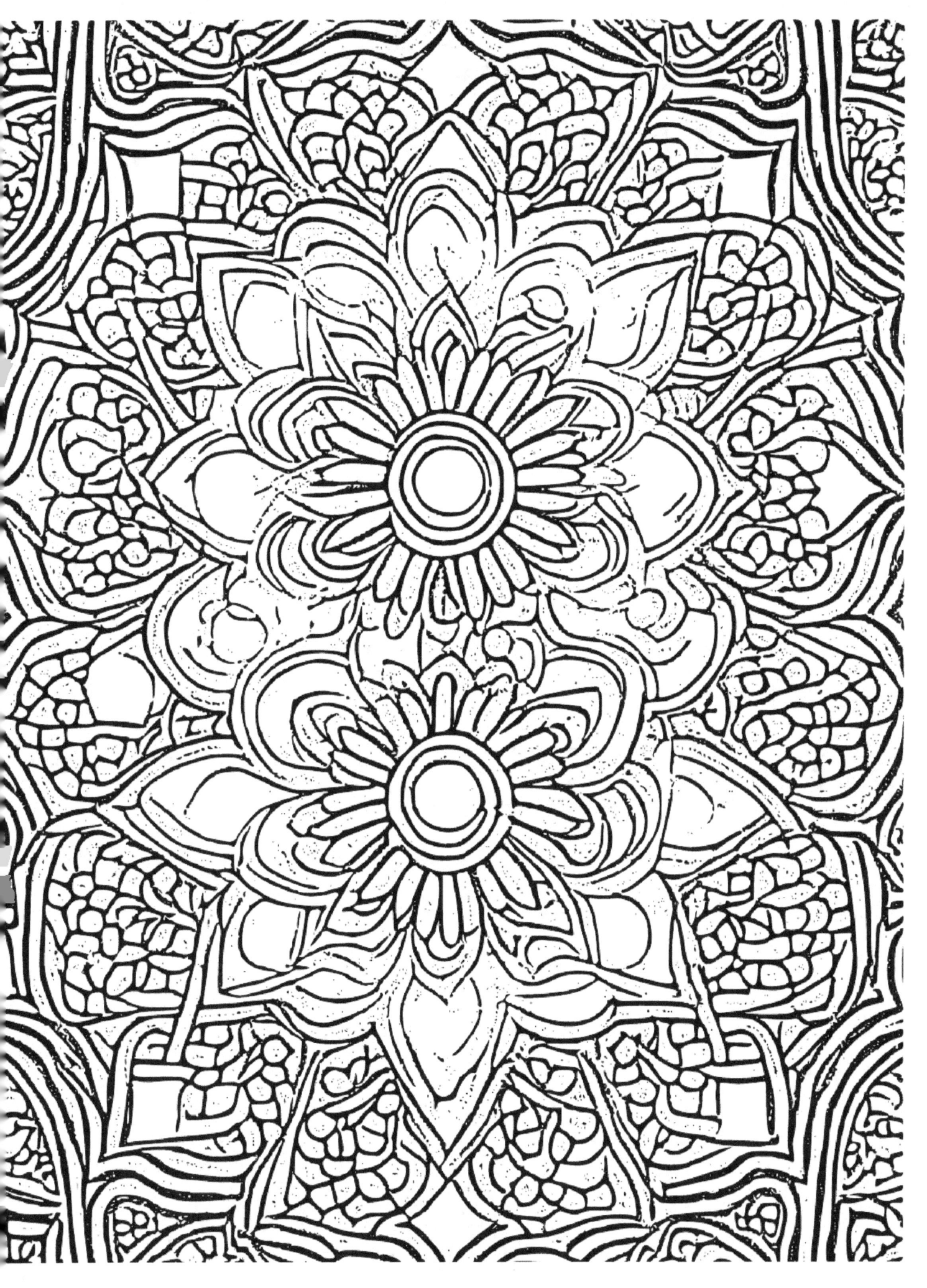

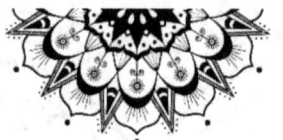

"Imagination is more important than knowledge." - Albert Einstein

Notes

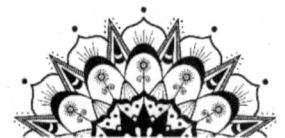

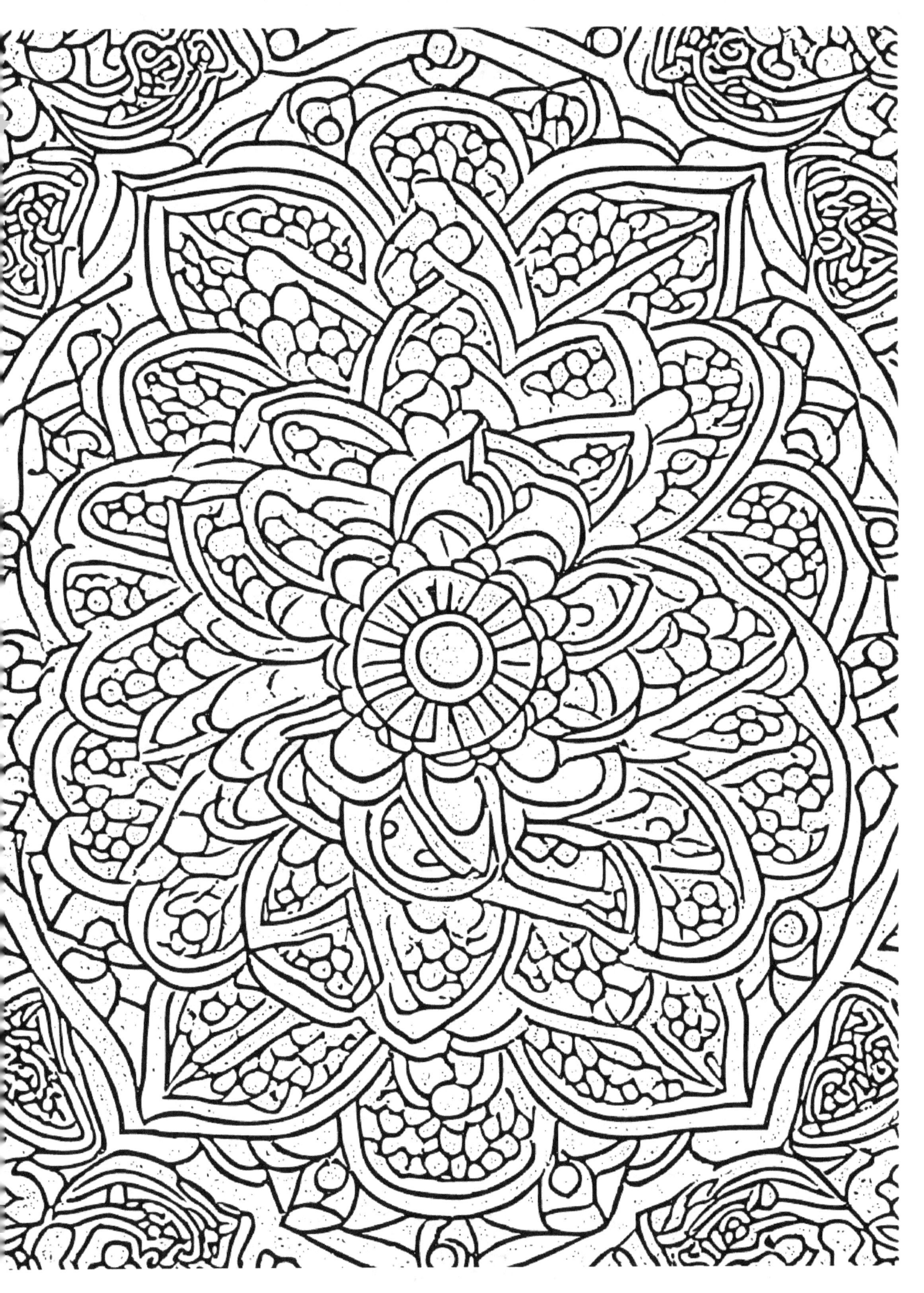

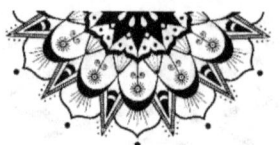

"The greatest glory in living lies not in never falling, but in rising every time we fall." - Nelson Mandela

Notes

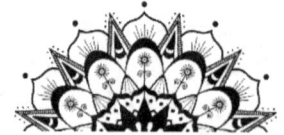

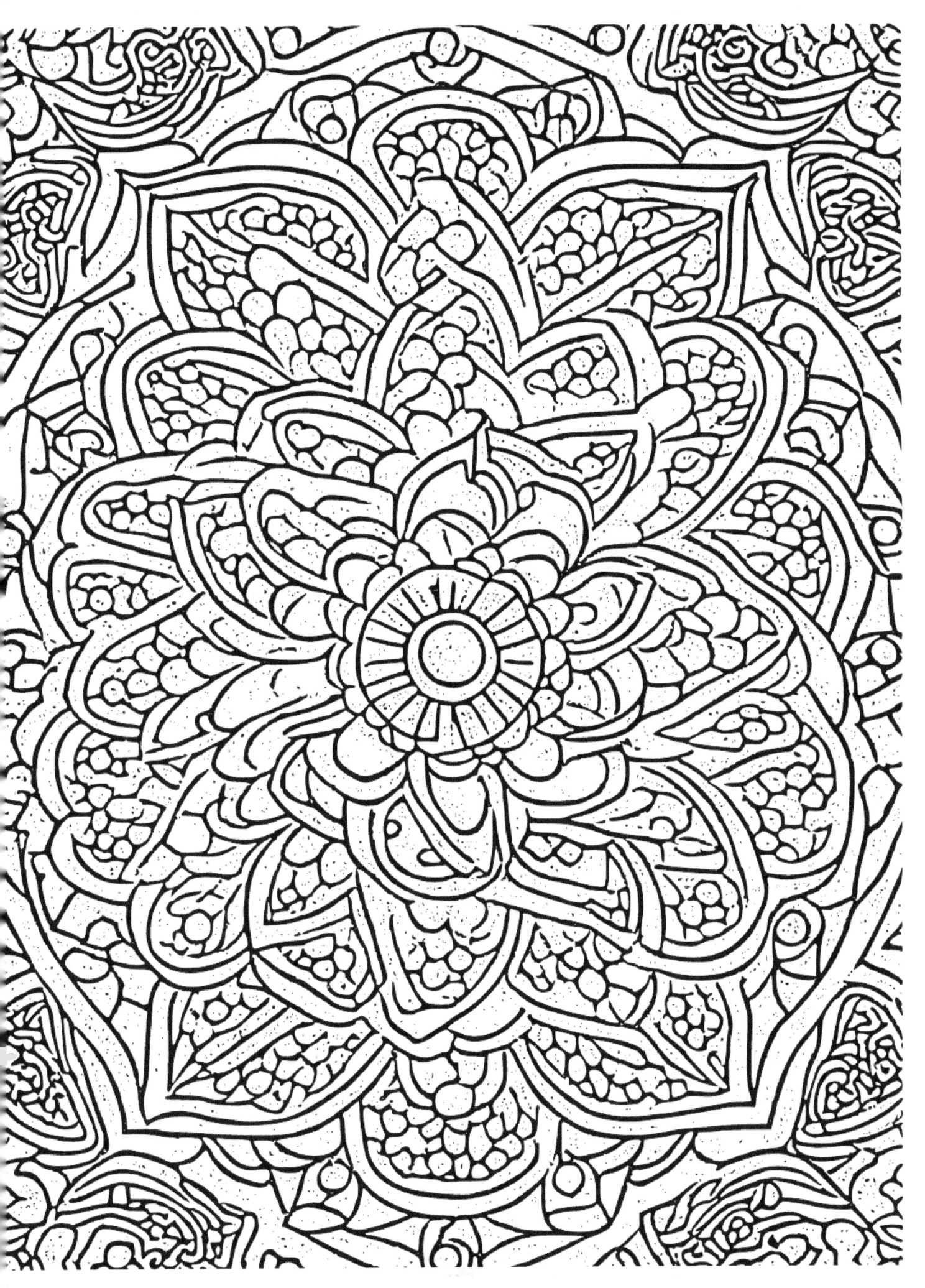

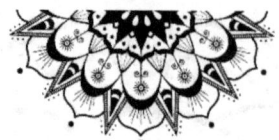

"Life is 10% what happens to me and 90% how I react to it." - Charles R. Swindoll

Notes

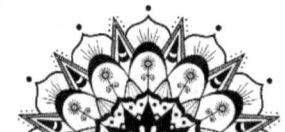

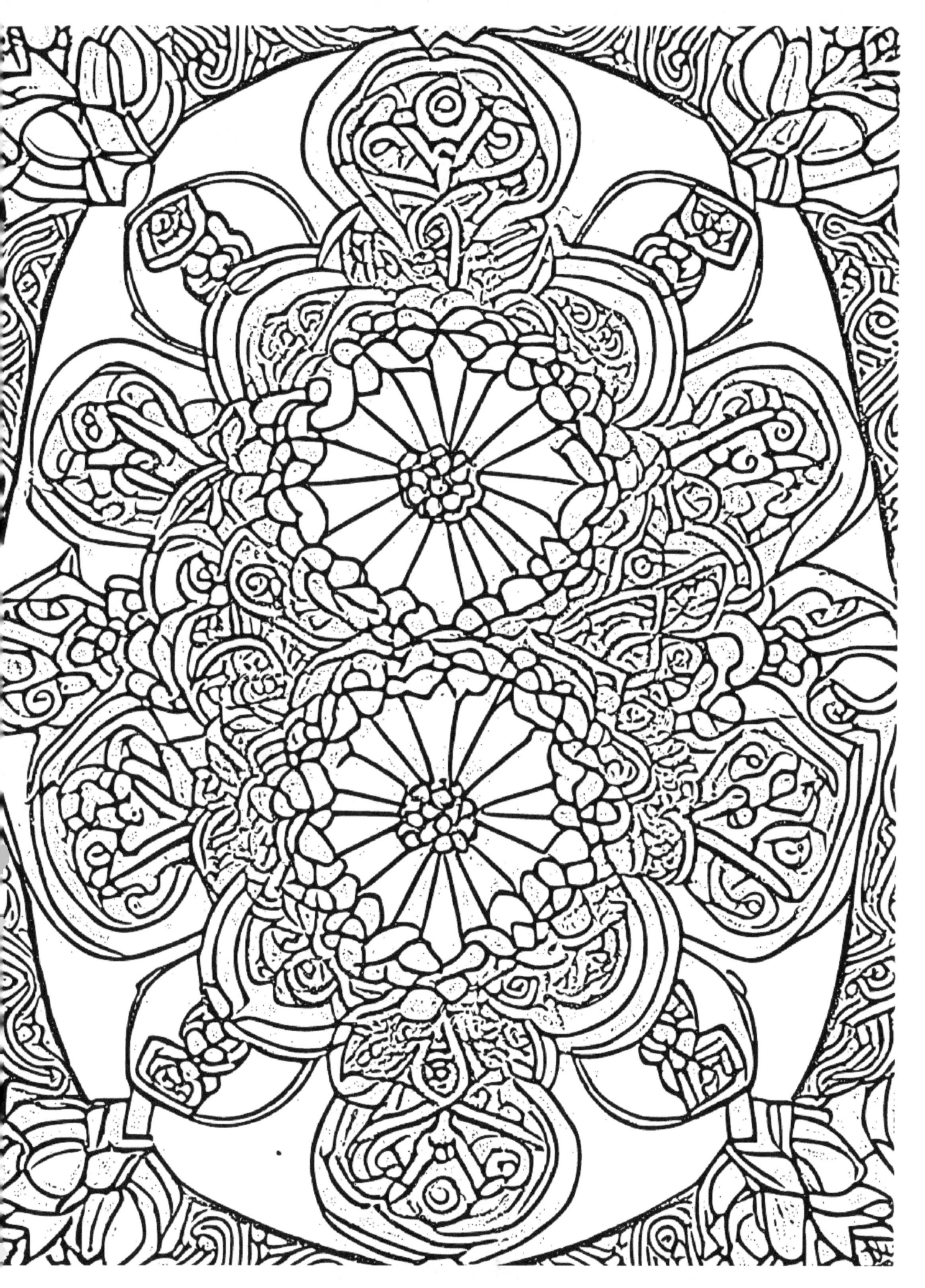

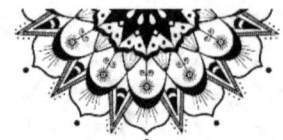

"Education is the most powerful weapon which you can use to change the world." - Nelson Mandela

Notes

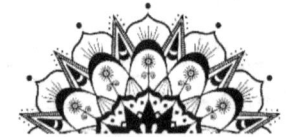

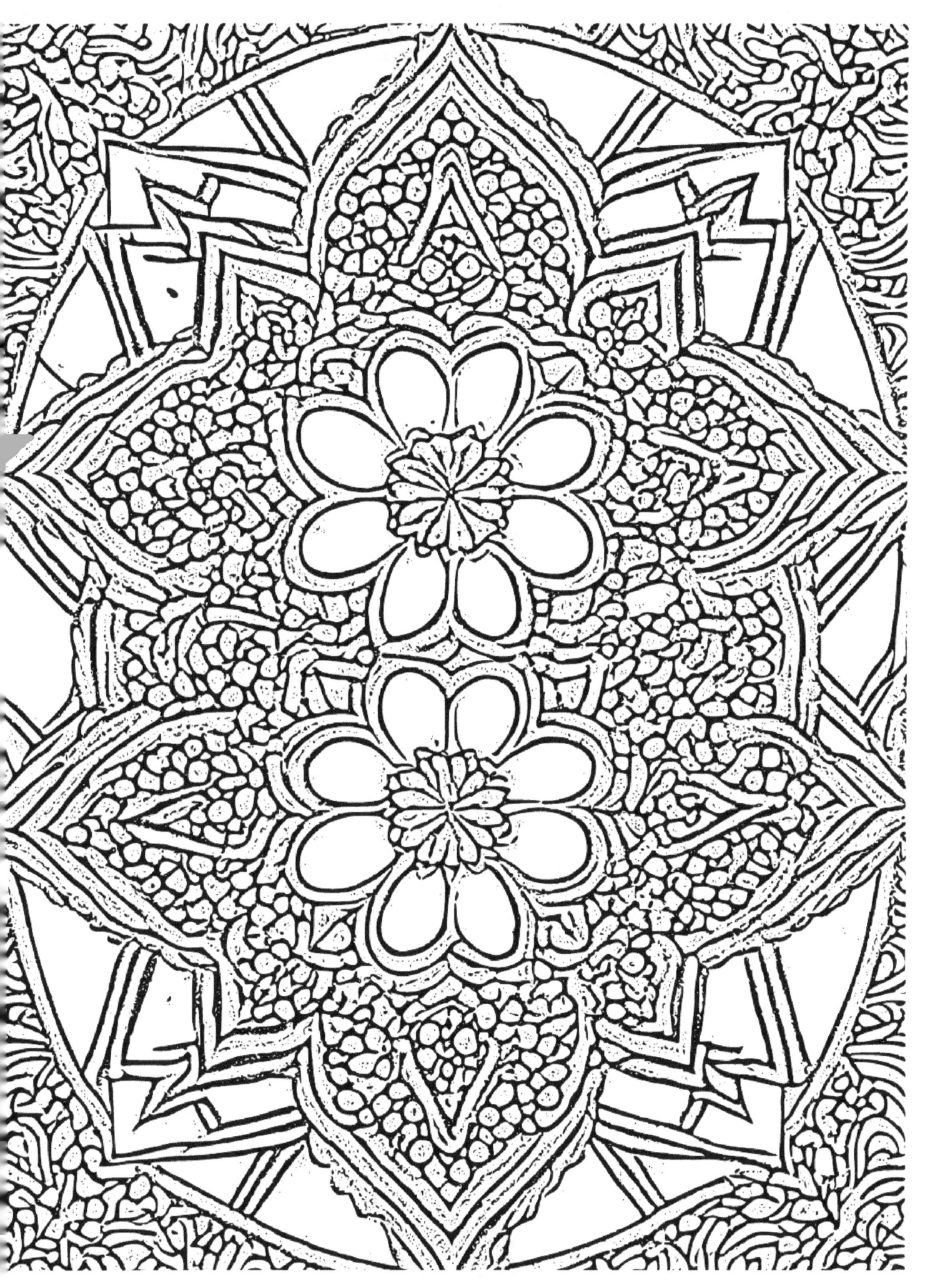

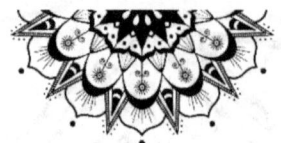

"Don't judge each day by the harvest you reap, but by the seeds that you plant."
– Robert Louis Stevenson

Notes

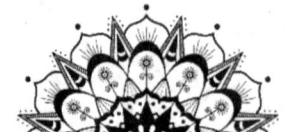

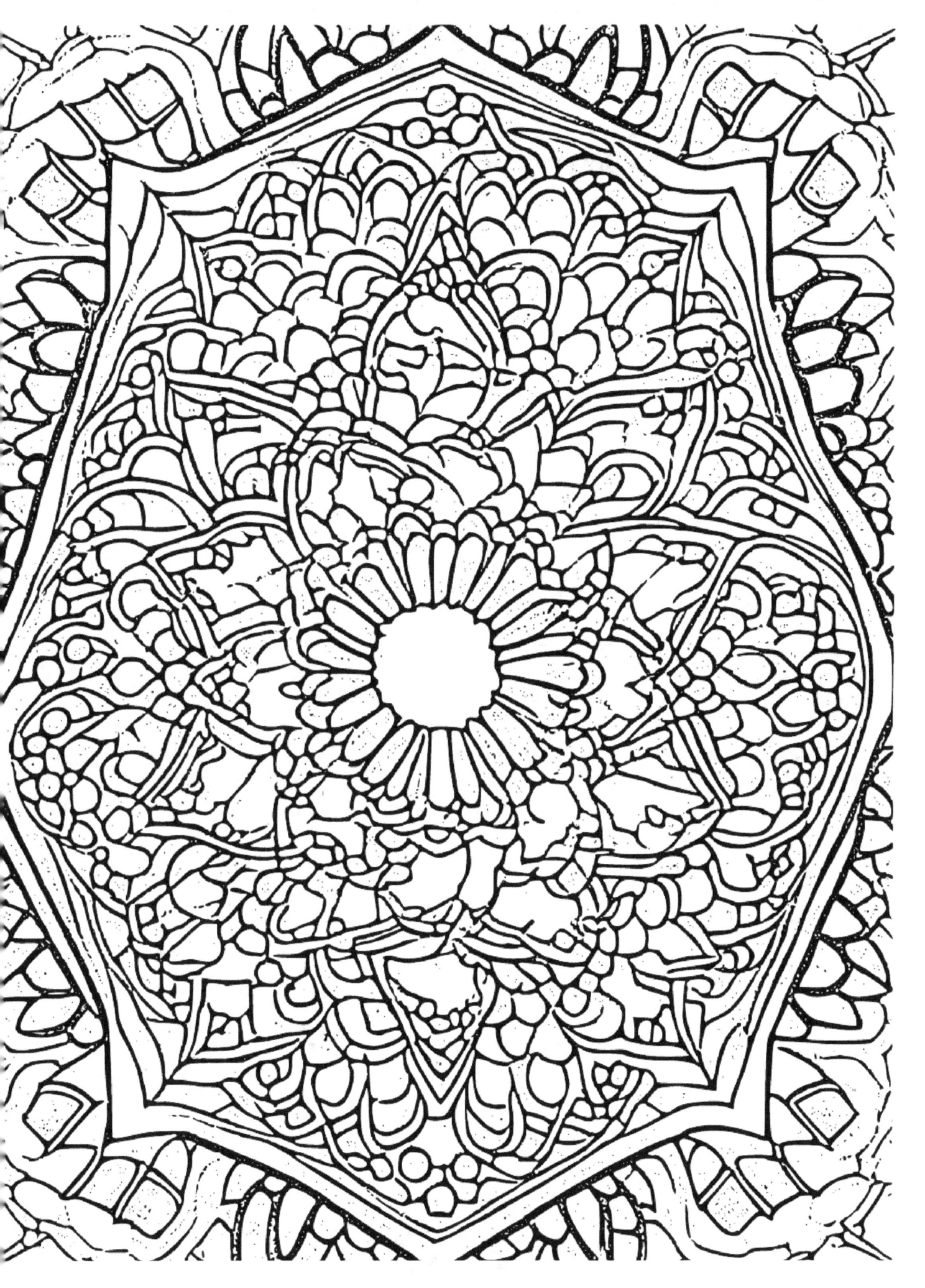

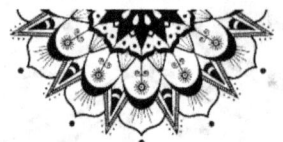

"Success is not the key to happiness. Happiness is the key to success. If you love what you are doing, you will be successful." - Albert Schweitzer

Notes

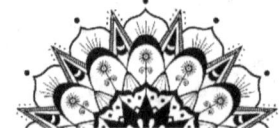

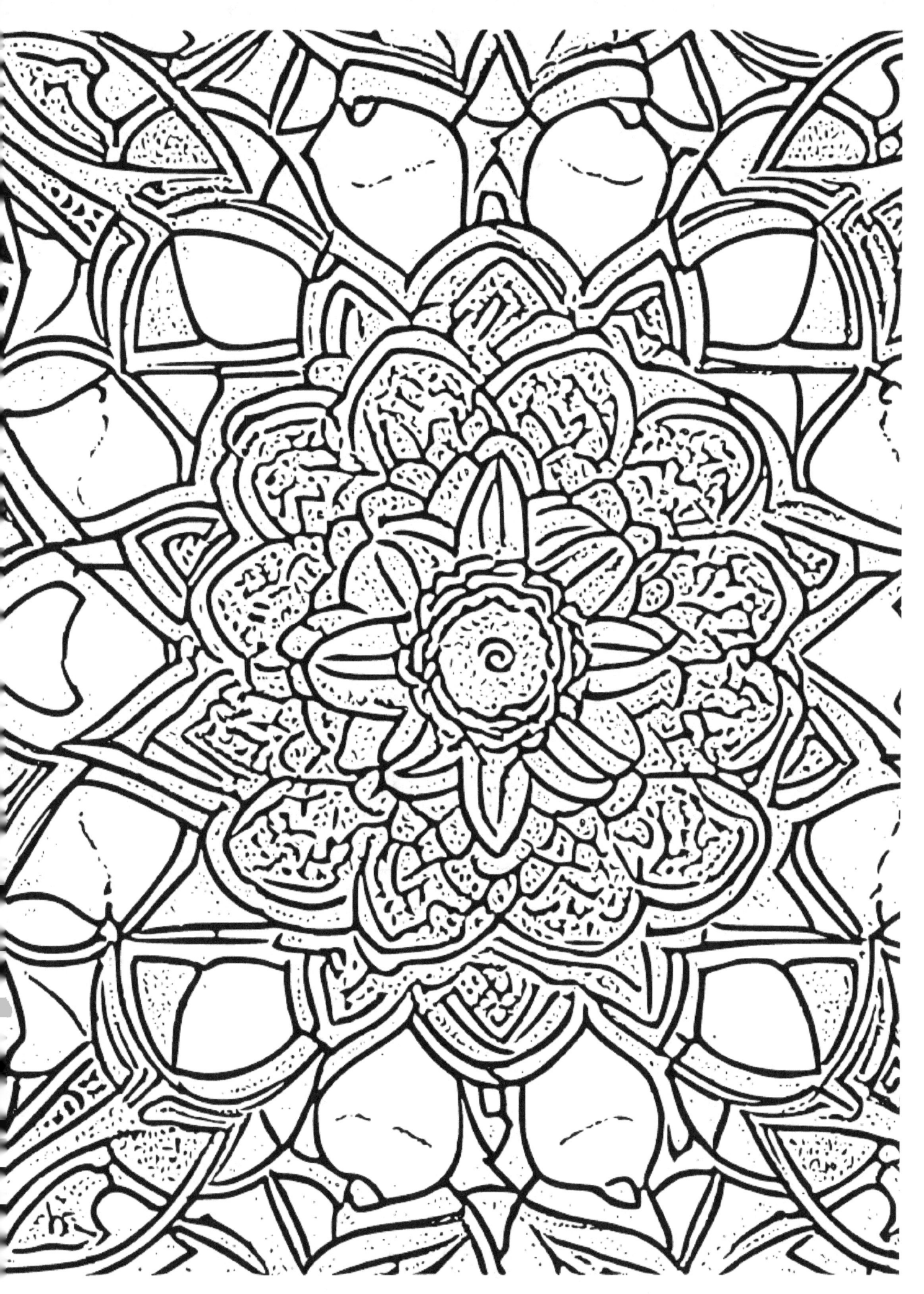

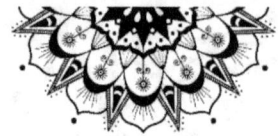

"The true measure of a man is not found in how he behaves in moments of comfort and convenience, but how he stands at times of controversy and challenges." - Martin Luther King Jr.

Notes

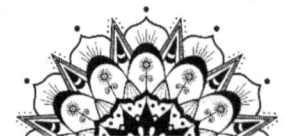

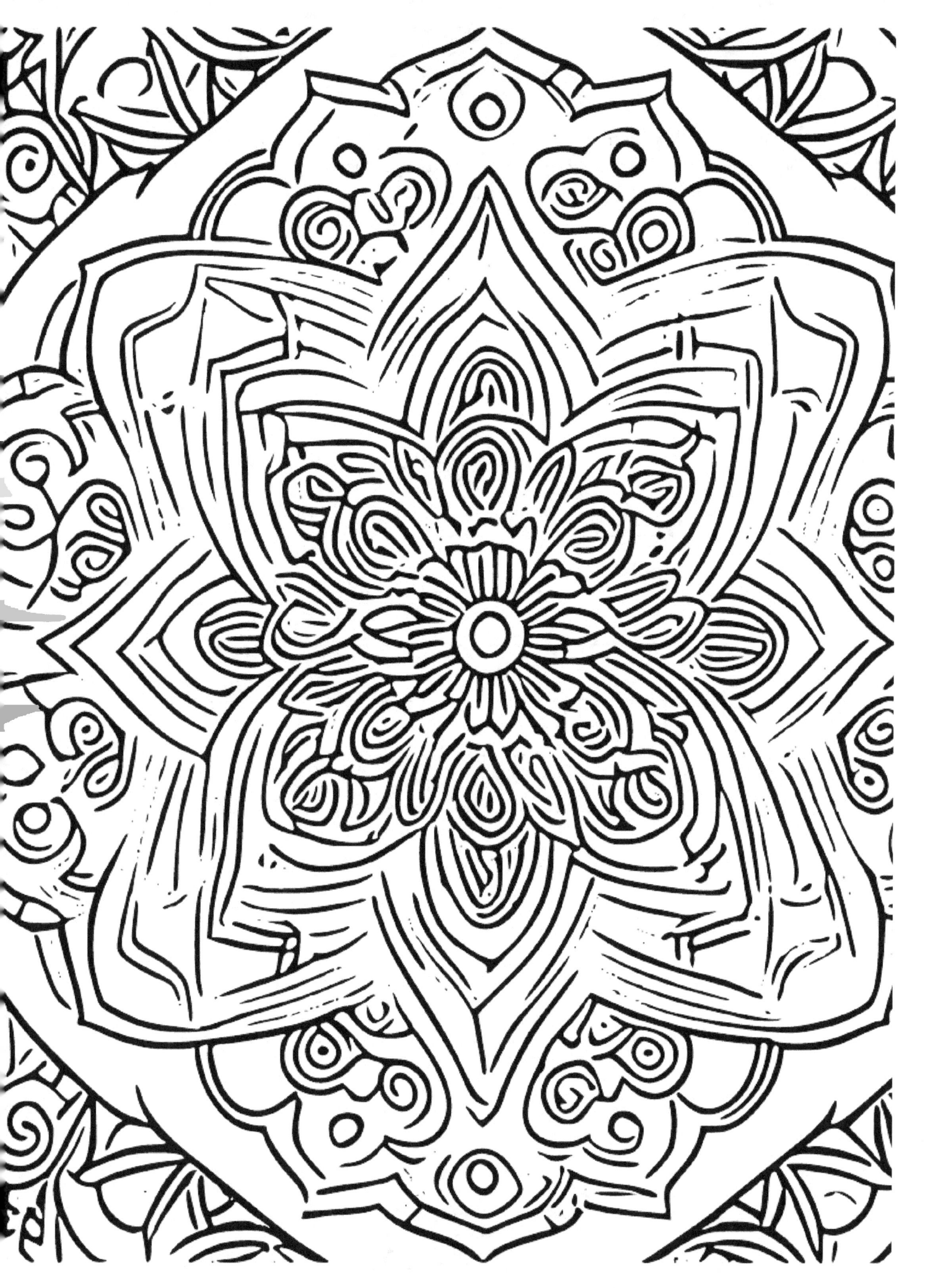

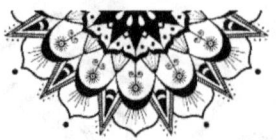

"Time is too slow for those who wait, too swift for those who fear, too long for those who grieve, too short for those who rejoice. But for those who love, time is eternity." – Henry Van Dyke

Notes

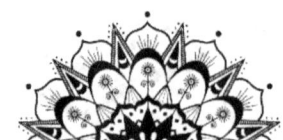

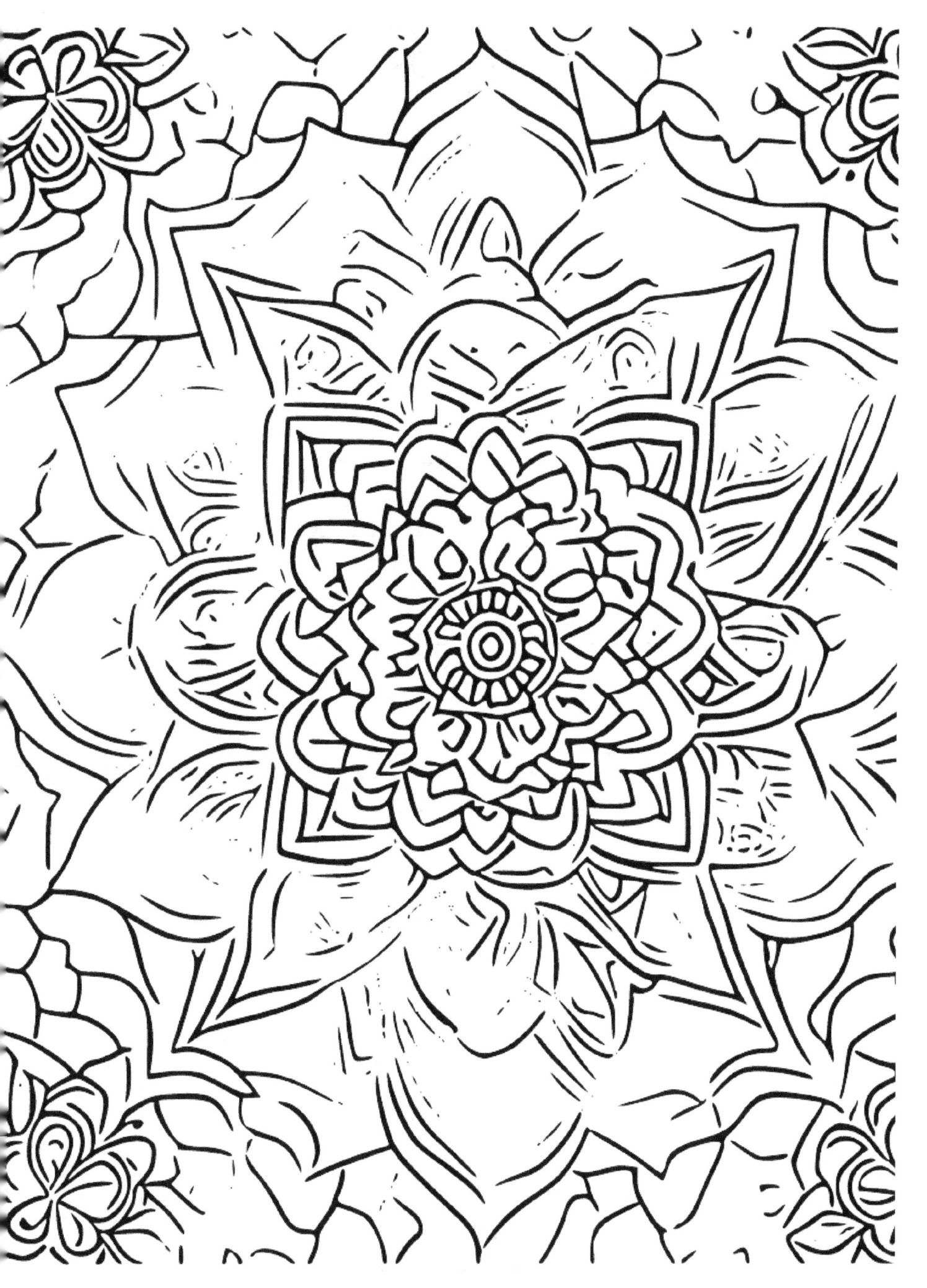

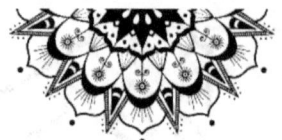

"Life isn't about finding yourself, it's about creating yourself." - George Bernard Shaw

Notes

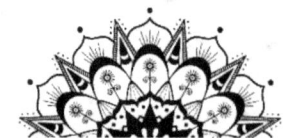

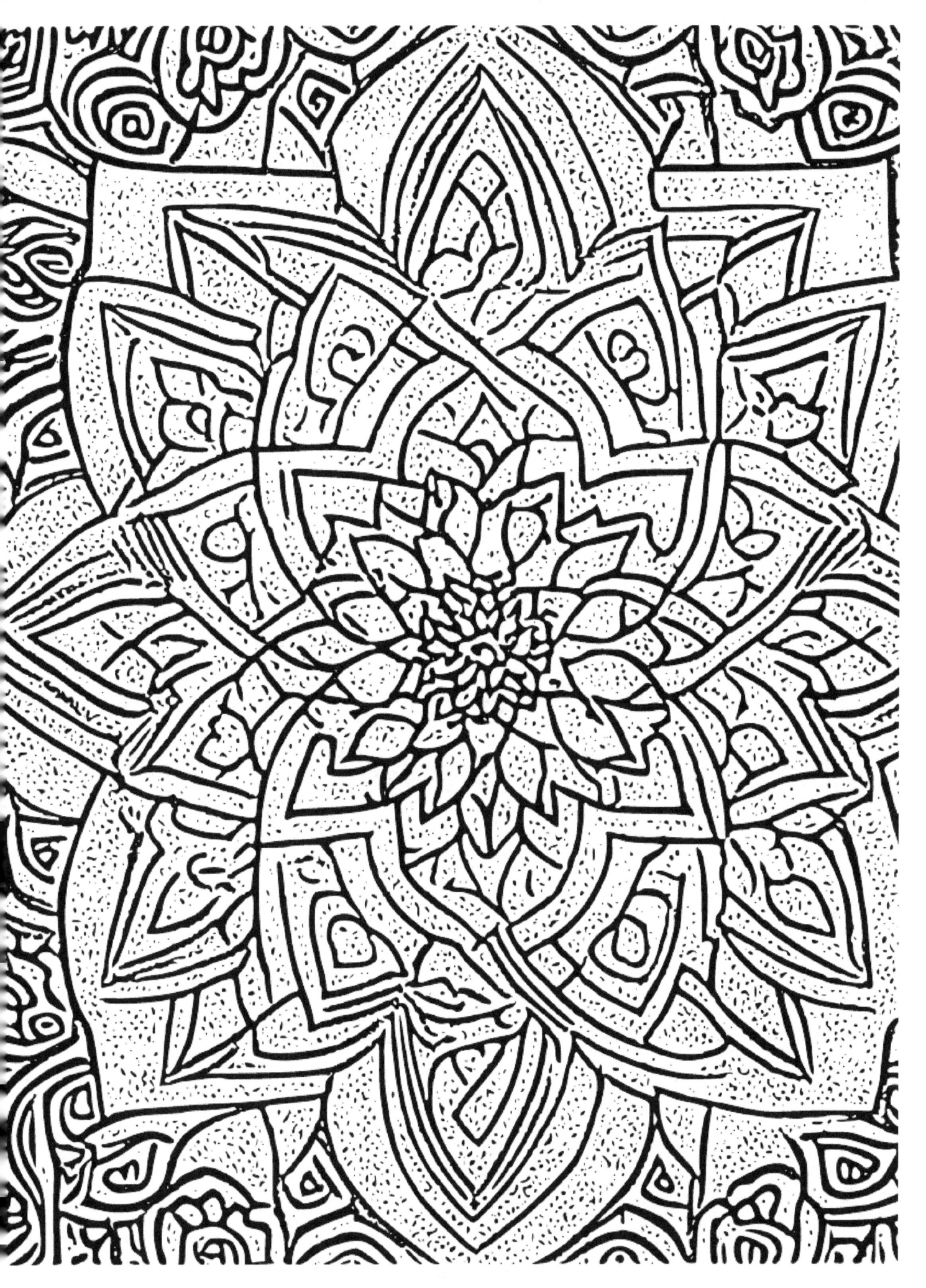

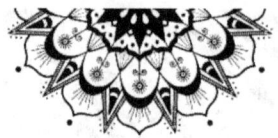

"The pessimist complains about the wind; the optimist expects it to change; the realist adjusts the sails." - William Arthur Ward

Notes

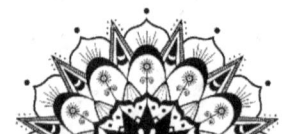

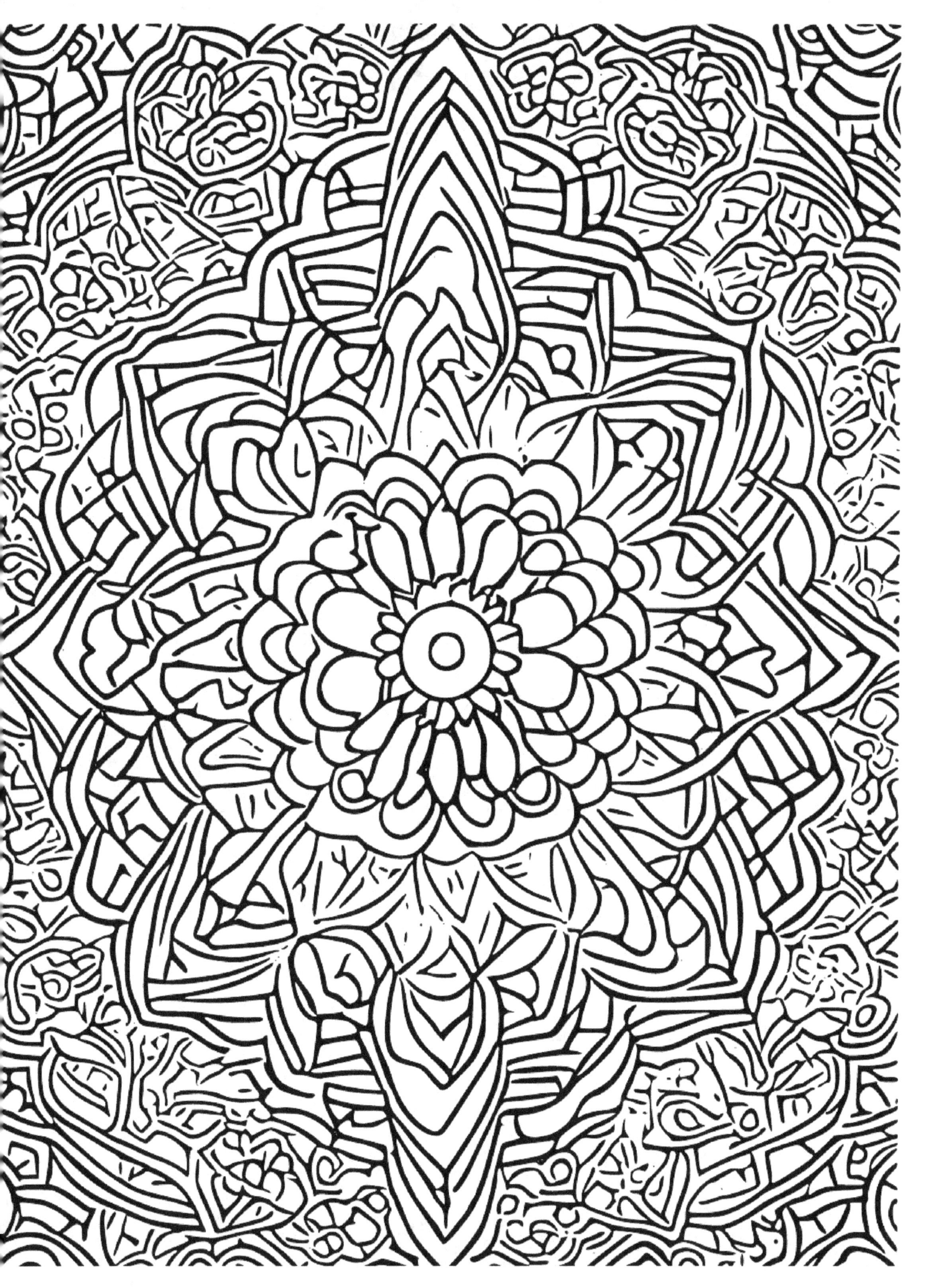

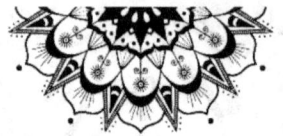

"Happiness is not something you postpone for the future; it's something you design for the present."
- Jim Rohn

Notes

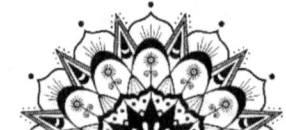

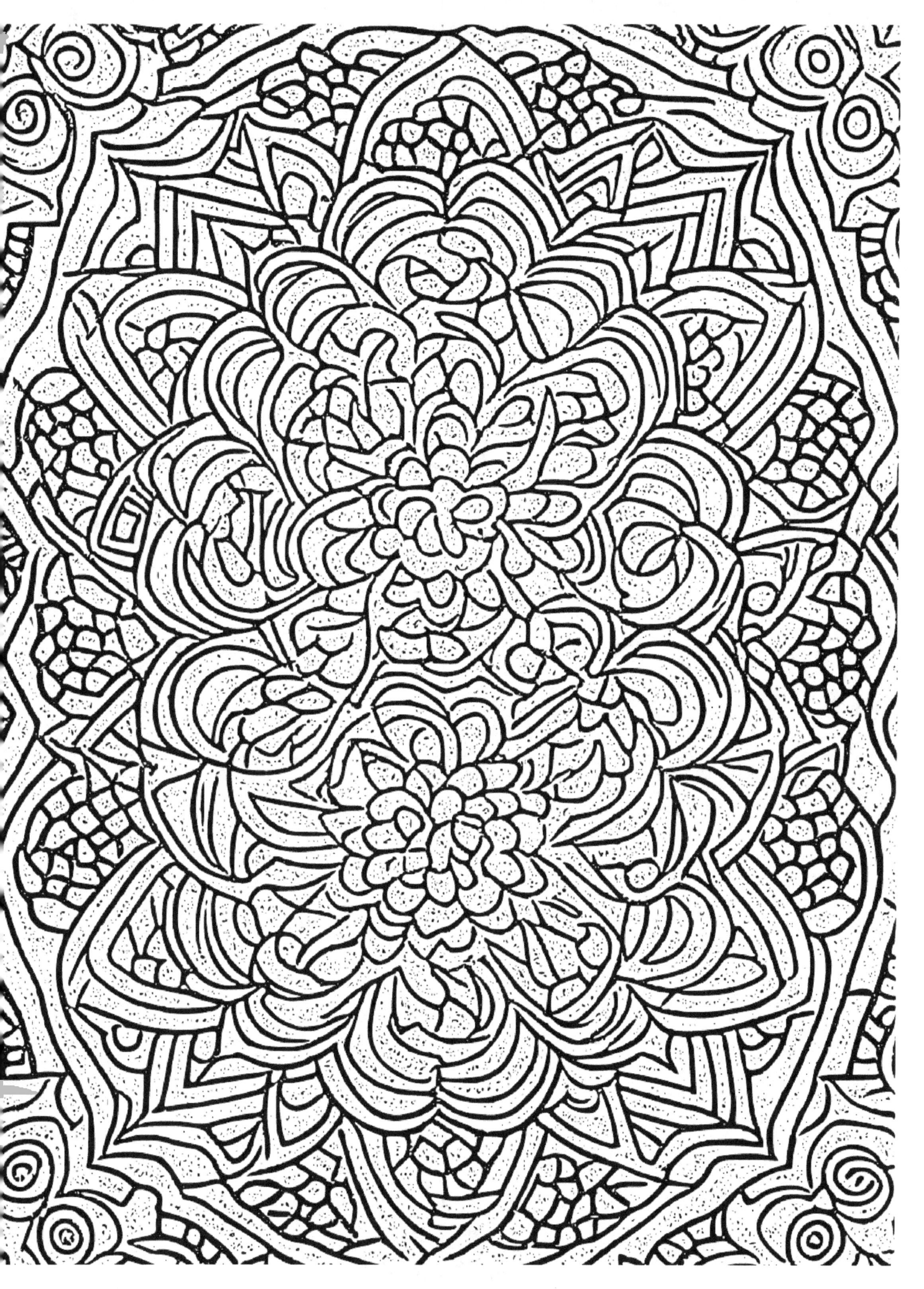

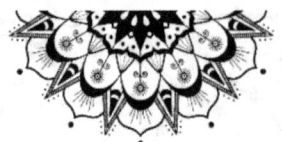

"The greatest mistake you can make in life is to be continually fearing you will make one."
- Elbert Hubbard

Notes

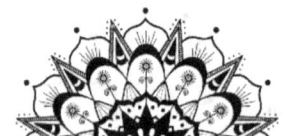

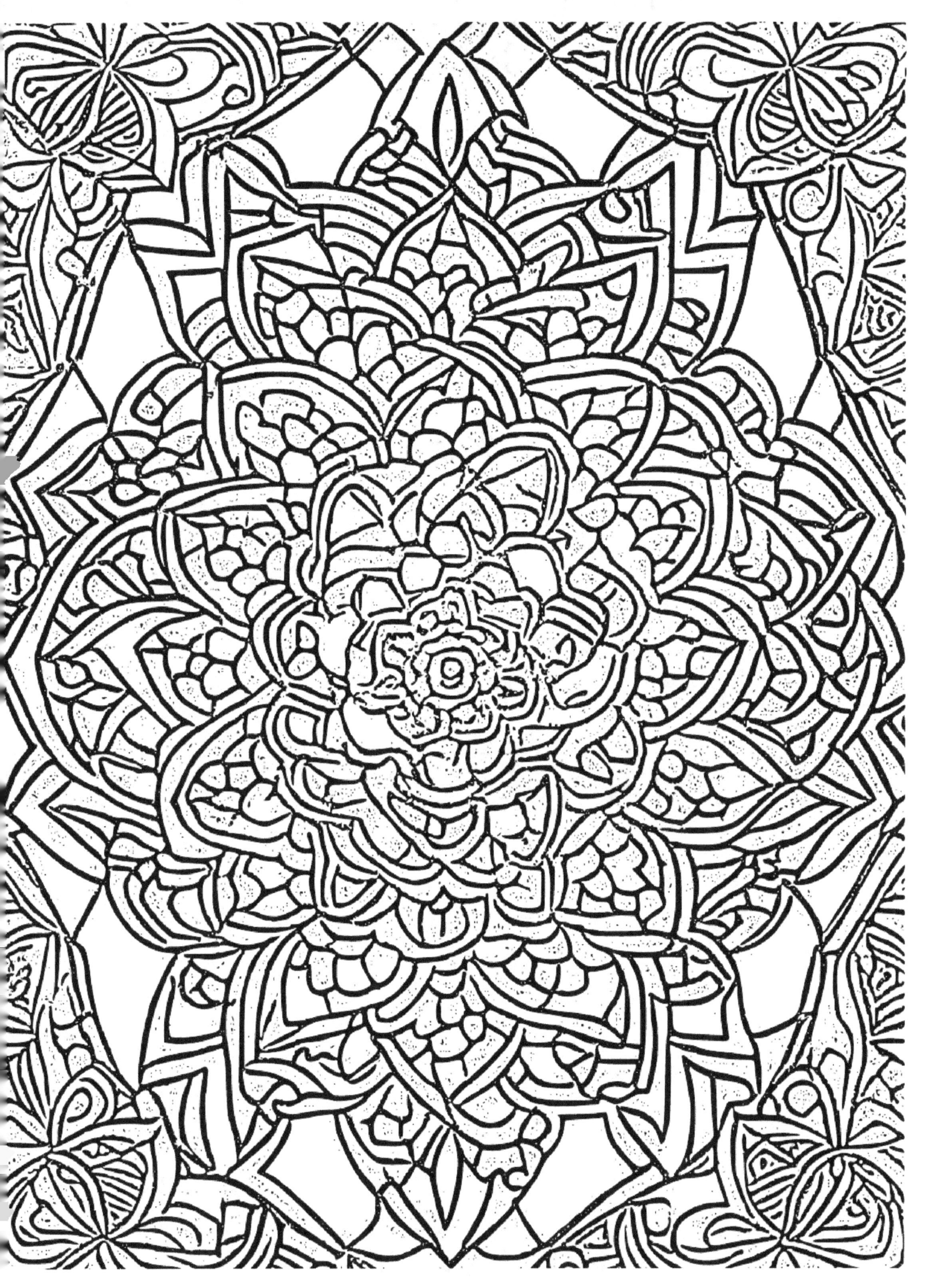

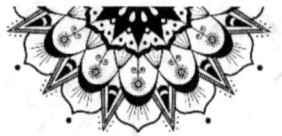

"Life is like riding a bicycle. To keep your balance, you must keep moving." - Albert Einstein

Notes

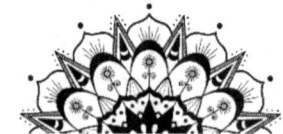

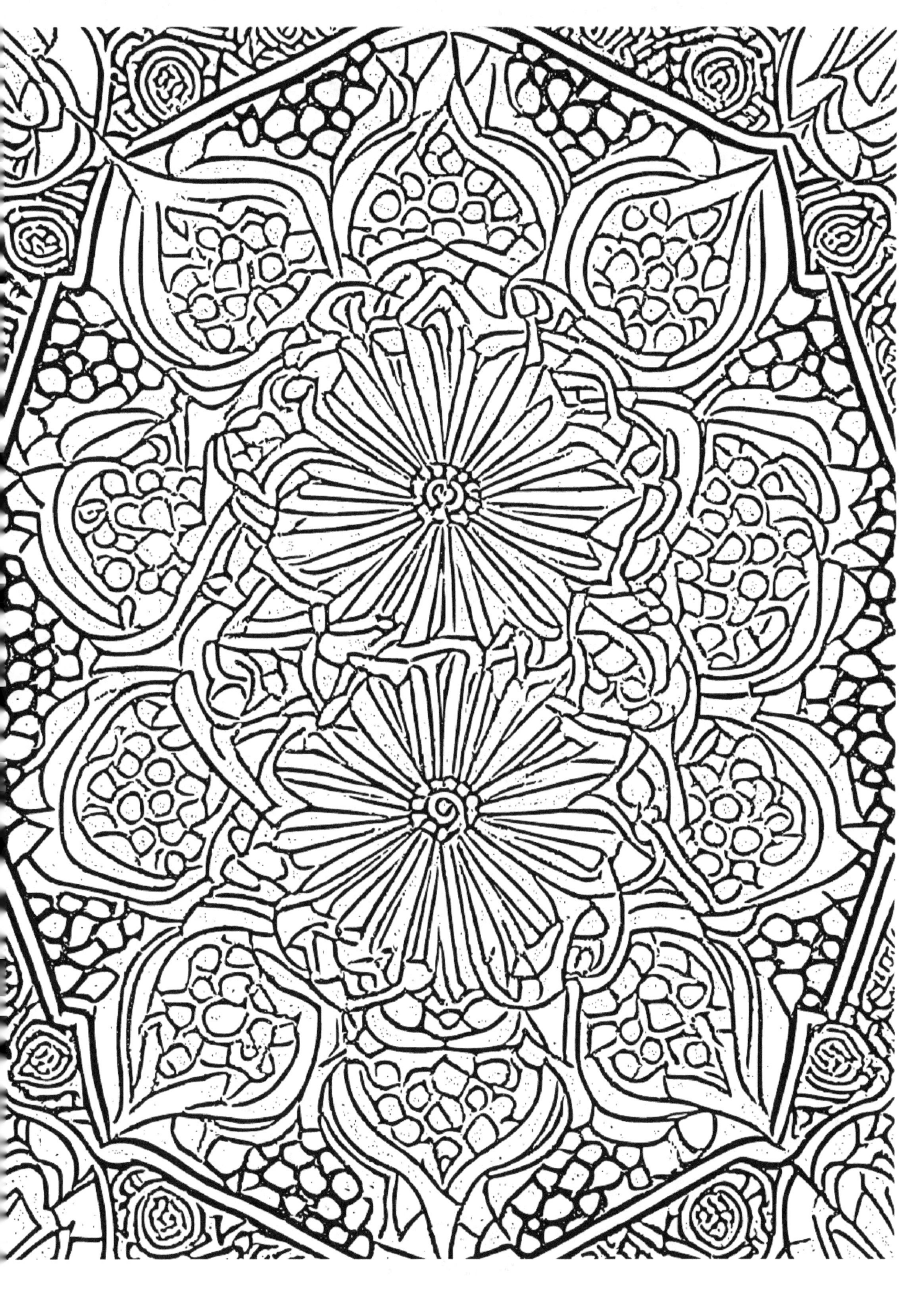

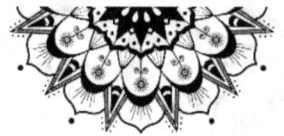

"Believe you can and you're halfway there." - Theodore Roosevelt

Notes

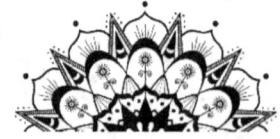

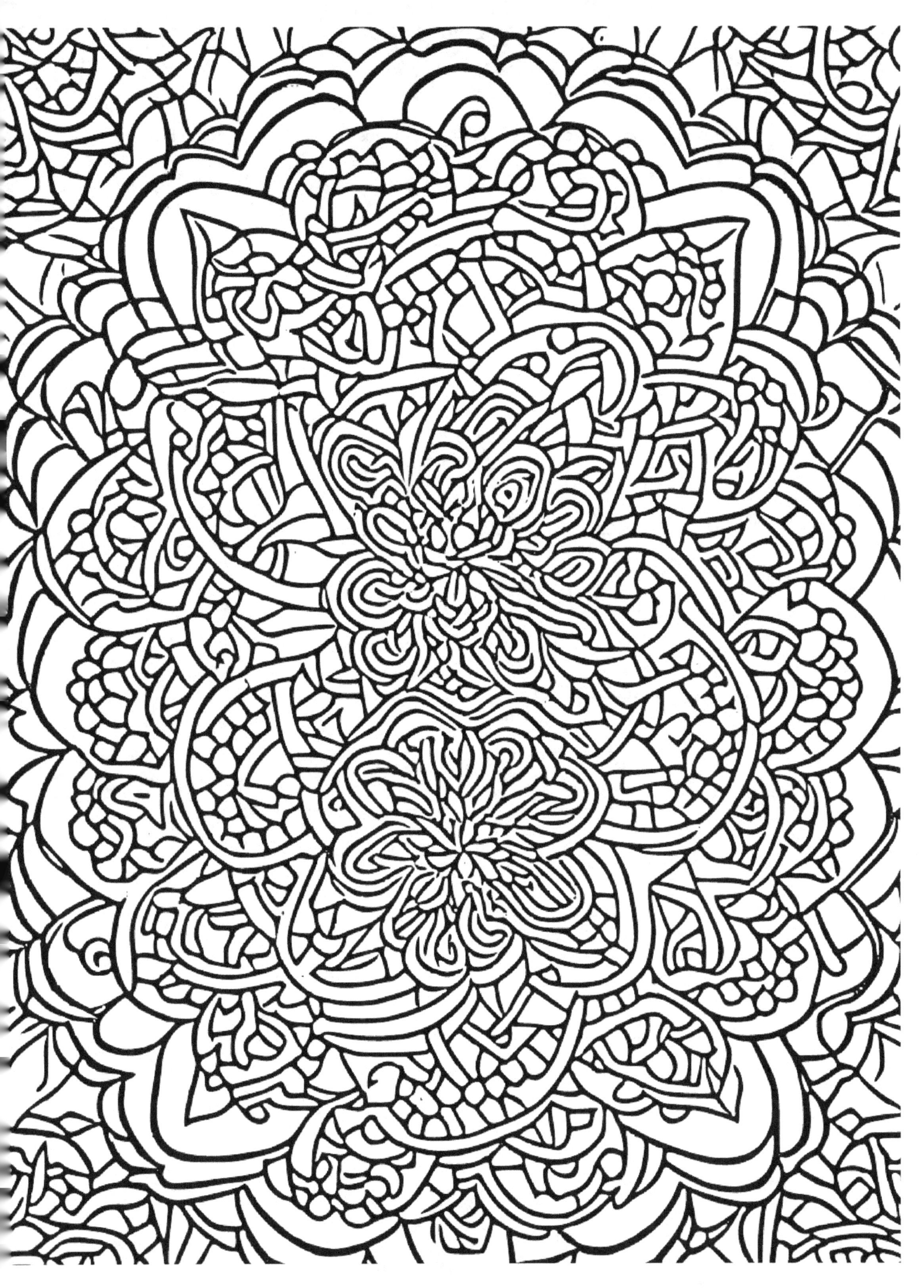

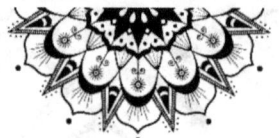

"The best preparation for tomorrow is doing your best today." - H. Jackson Brown Jr.

Notes

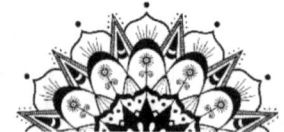

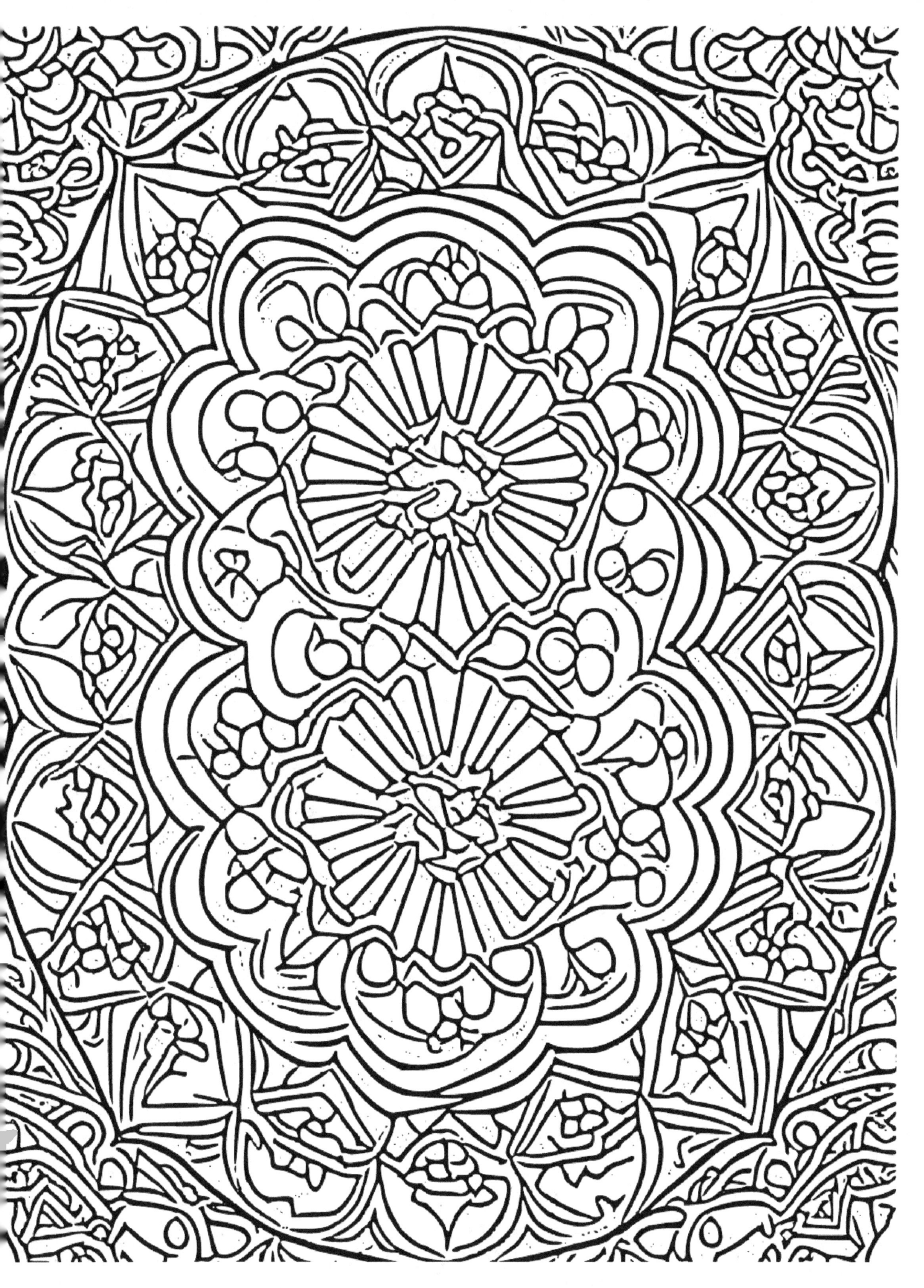

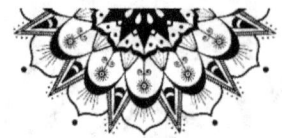

"It does not matter how slowly you go as long as you do not stop." - Confucius

Notes

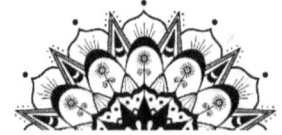

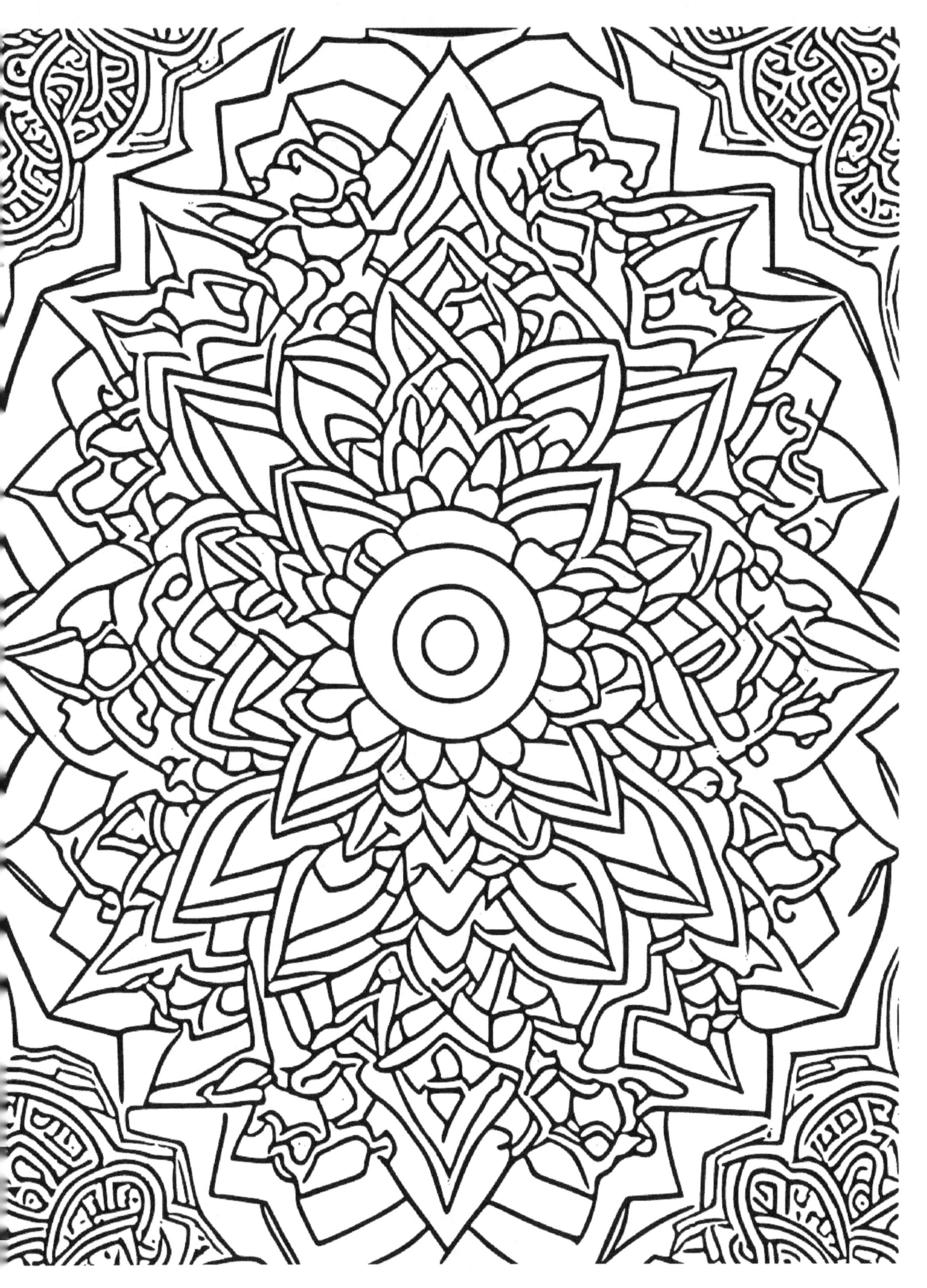

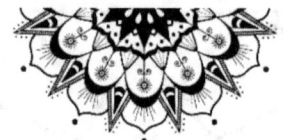

"The only person you should try to be better than is the person you were yesterday."
– Matty Mullins

Notes

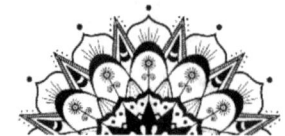

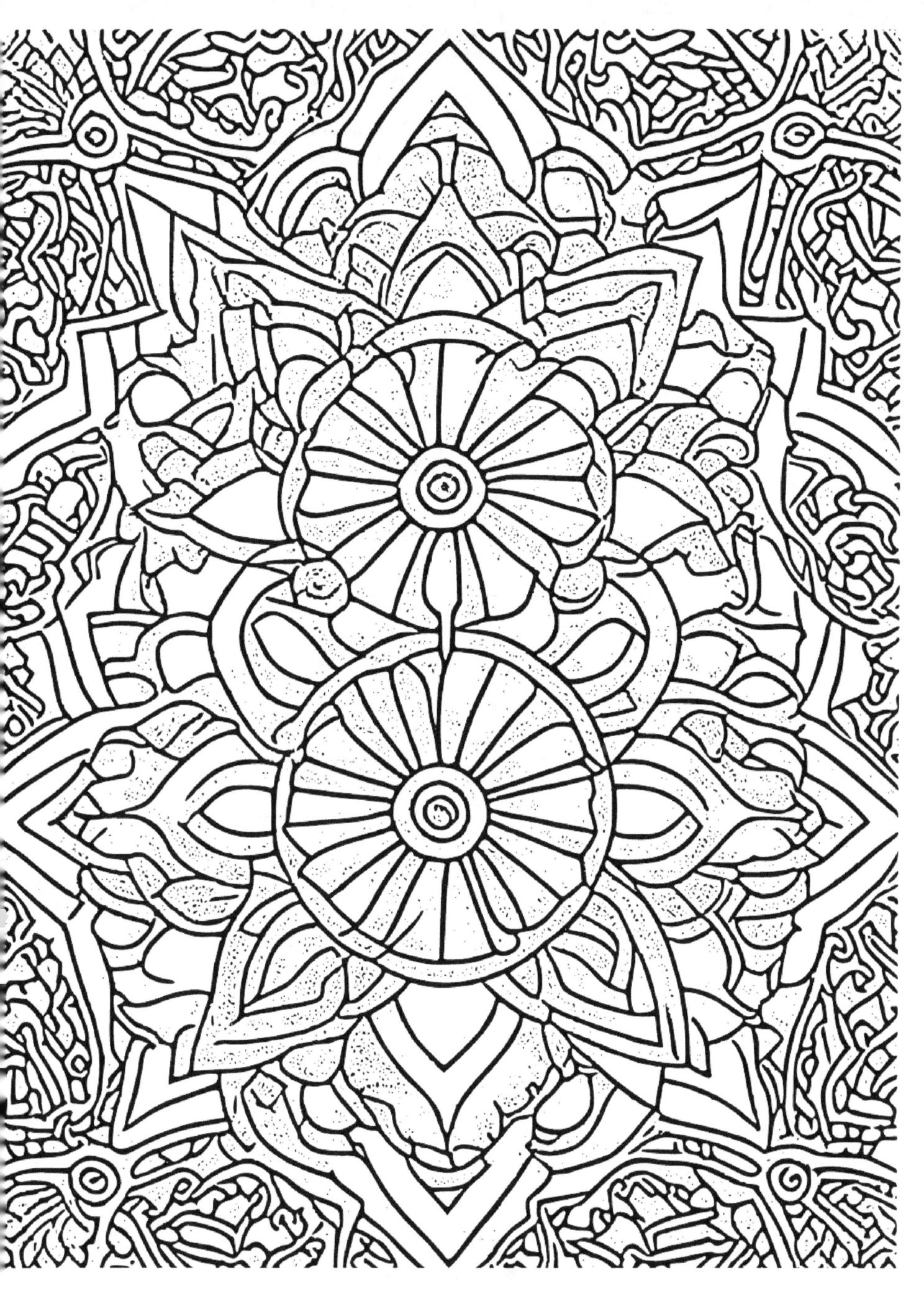

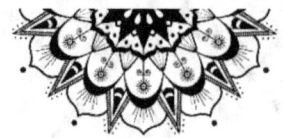

"The biggest risk is not taking any risk. In a world that's changing really quickly, the only strategy that is guaranteed to fail is not taking risks." - Mark Zuckerberg

Notes

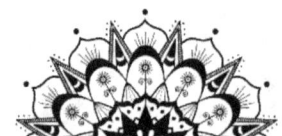

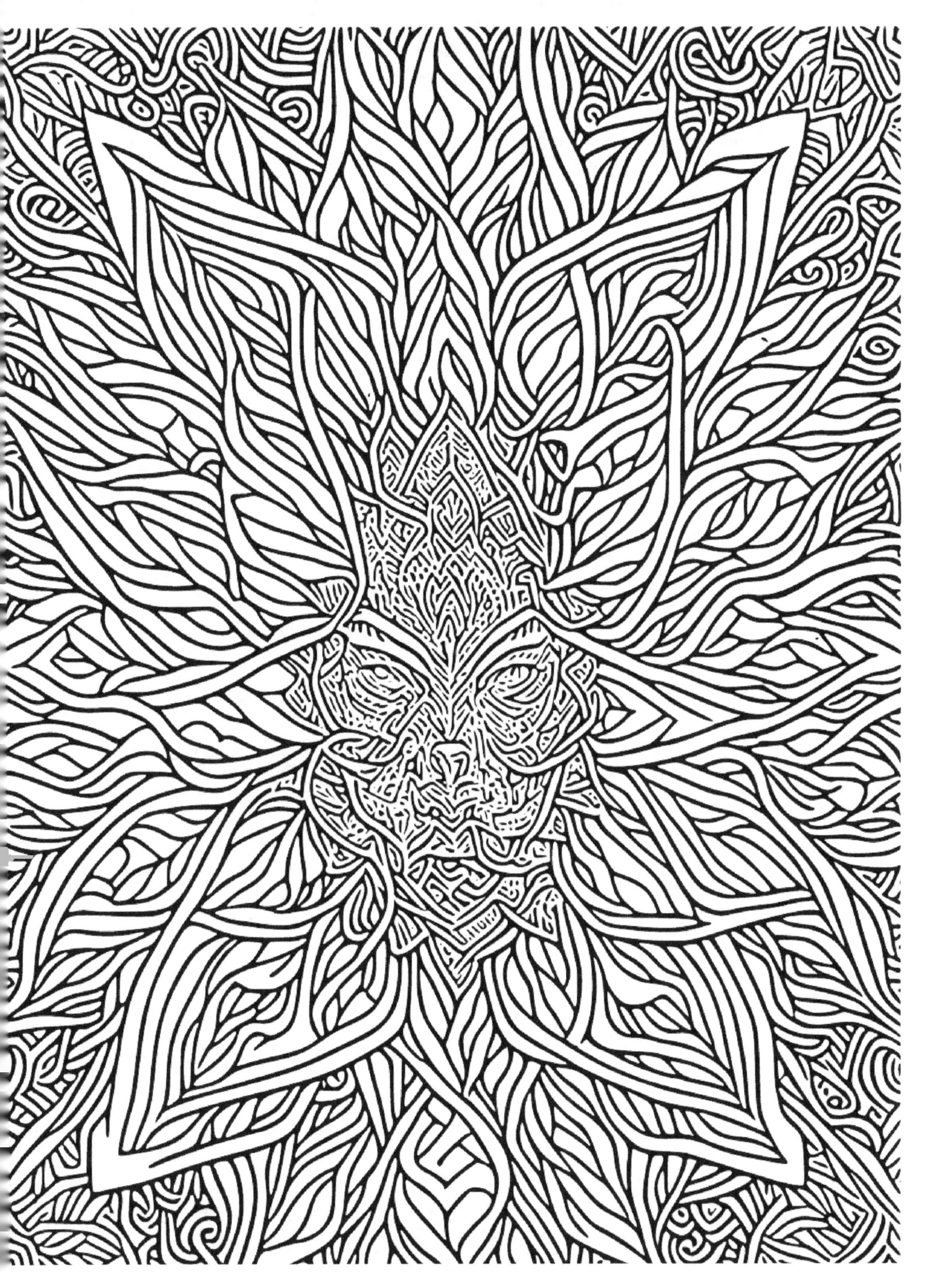

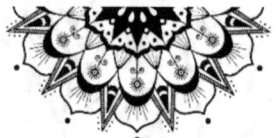

"Don't be afraid to give up the good to go for the great." - John D. Rockefeller

Notes

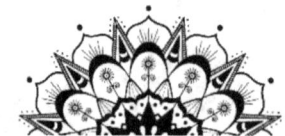

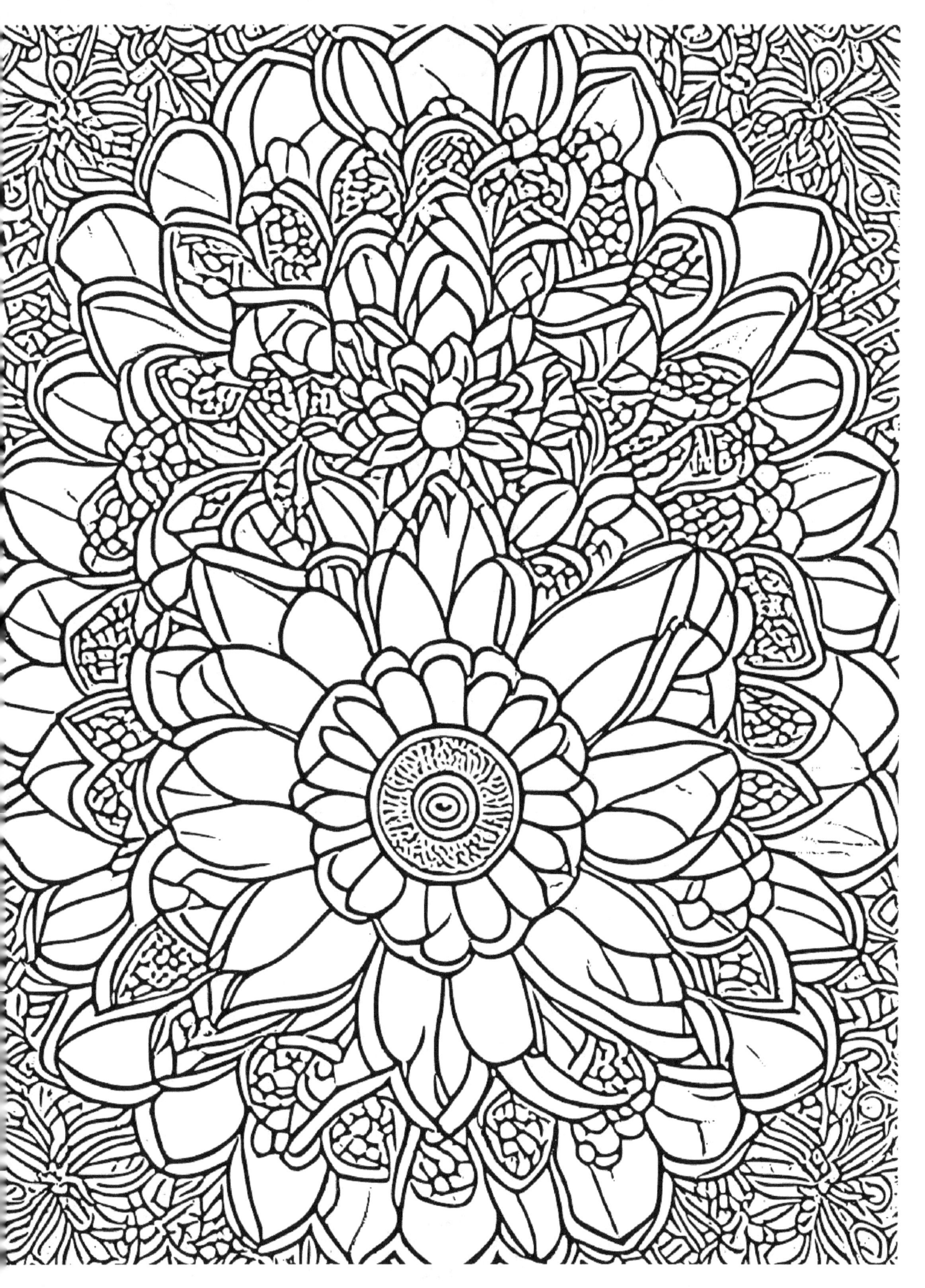

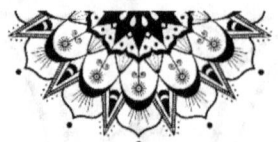

"You can't go back and change the beginning, but you can start where you are and change the ending." - C.S. Lewis

Notes

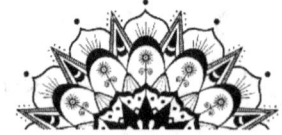

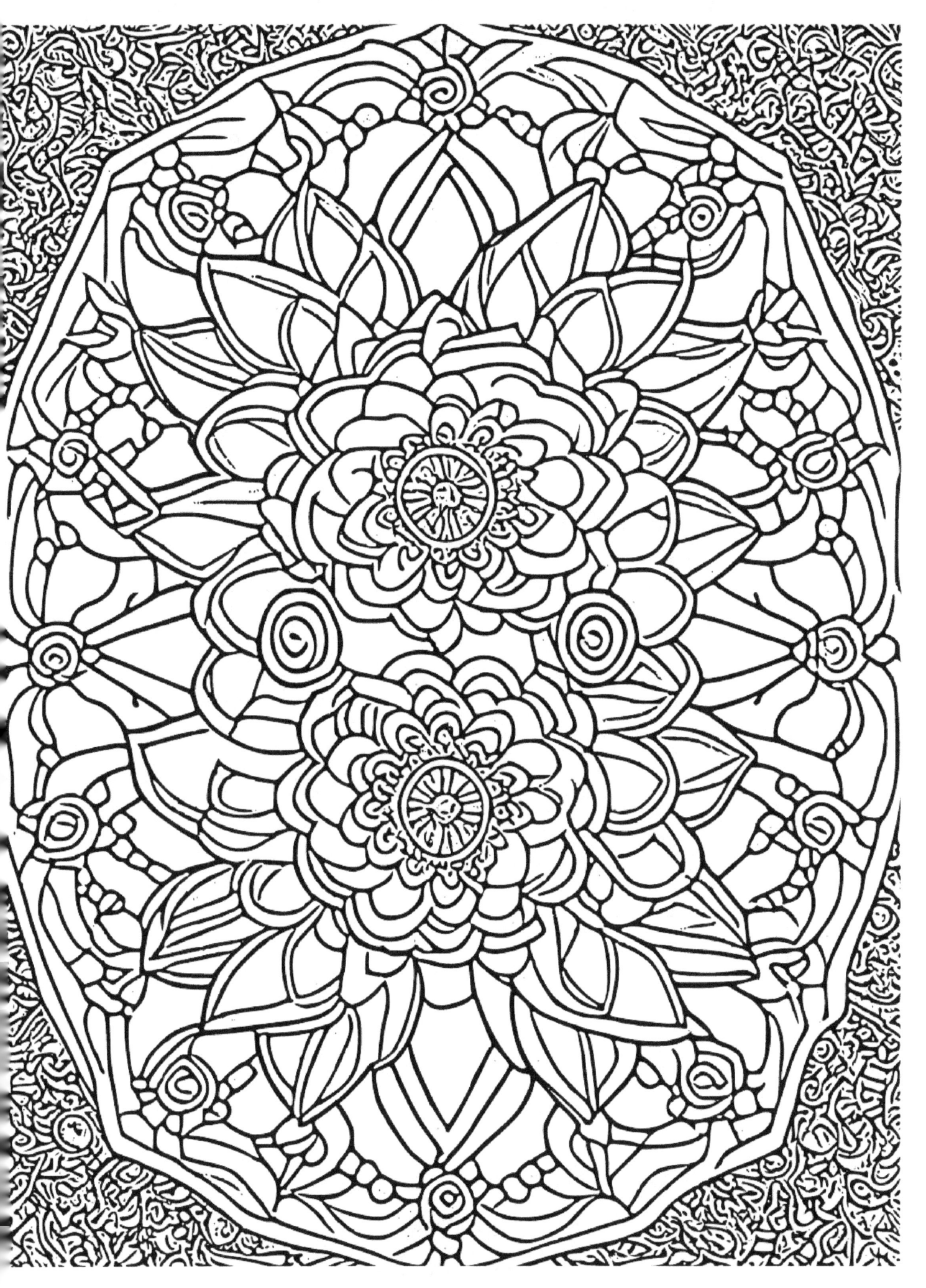

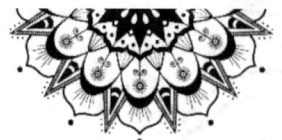

"Don't let yesterday take up too much of today." – Will Rogers

Notes

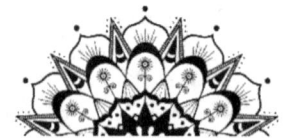

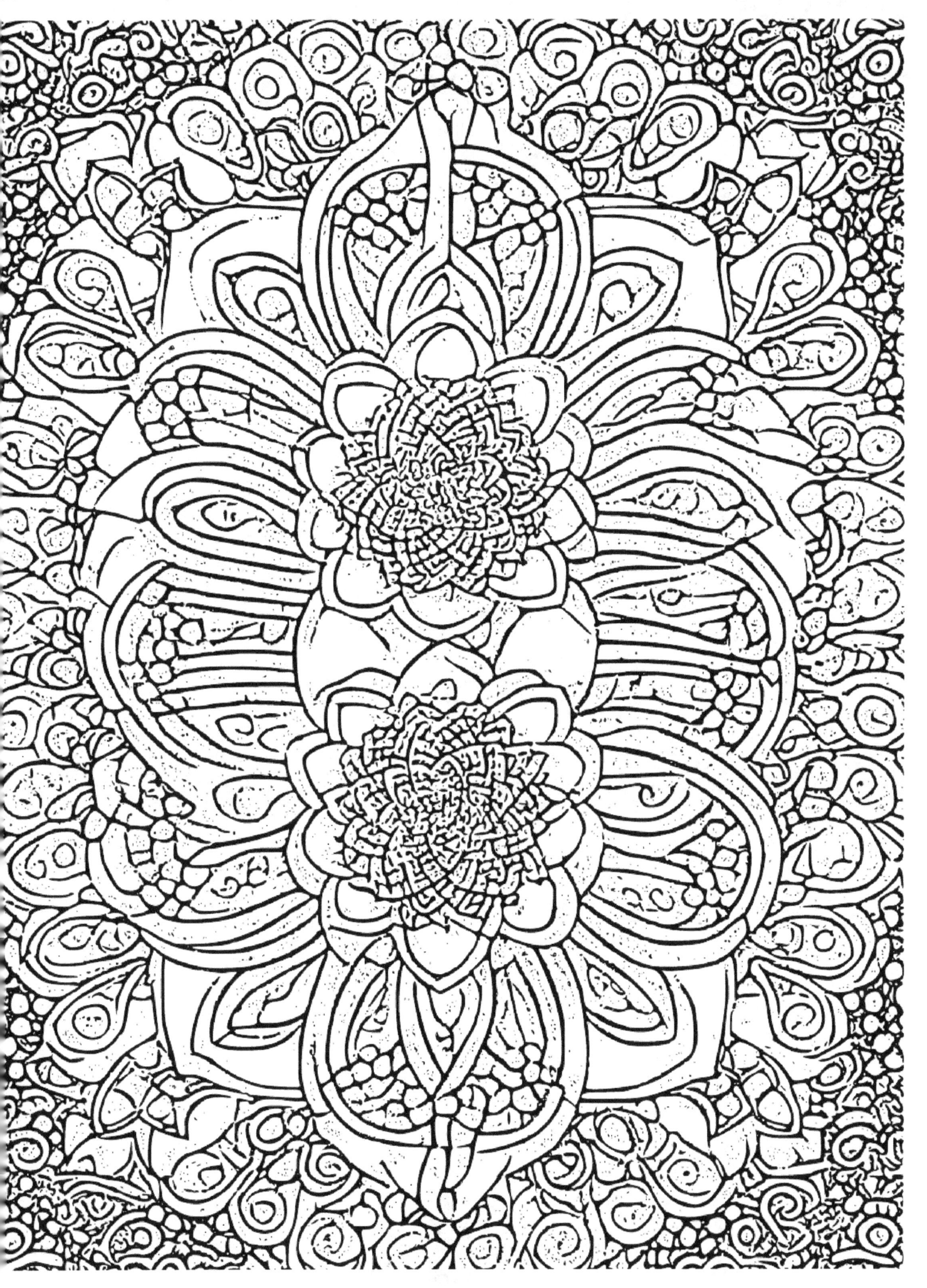

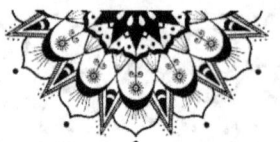

"The greatest wealth is to live content with little." - Plato

Notes

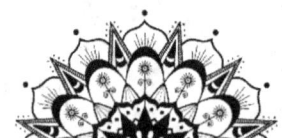

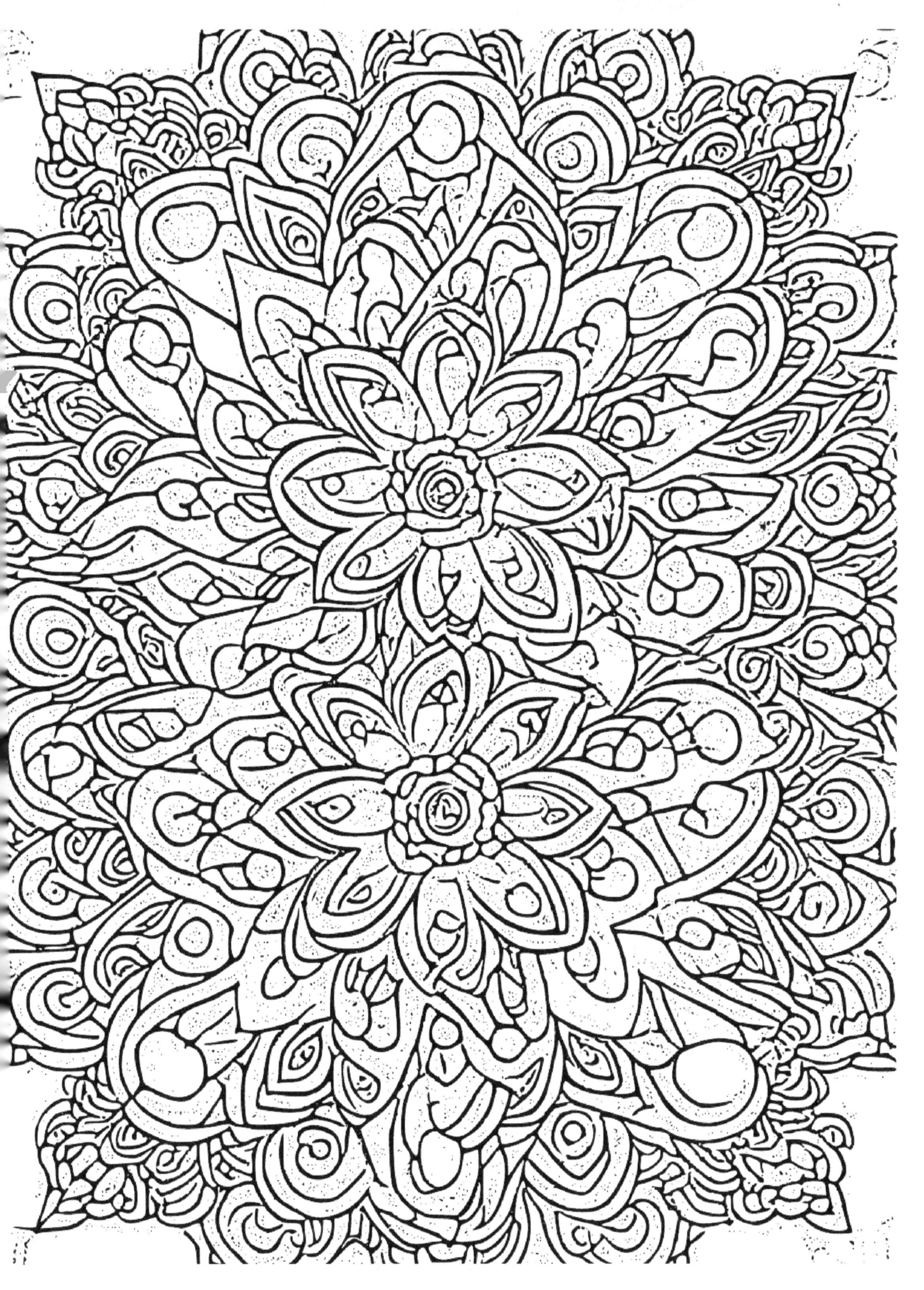

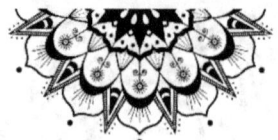

"The only thing necessary for the triumph of evil is for good men to do nothing." - Edmund Burke

Notes

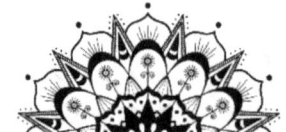

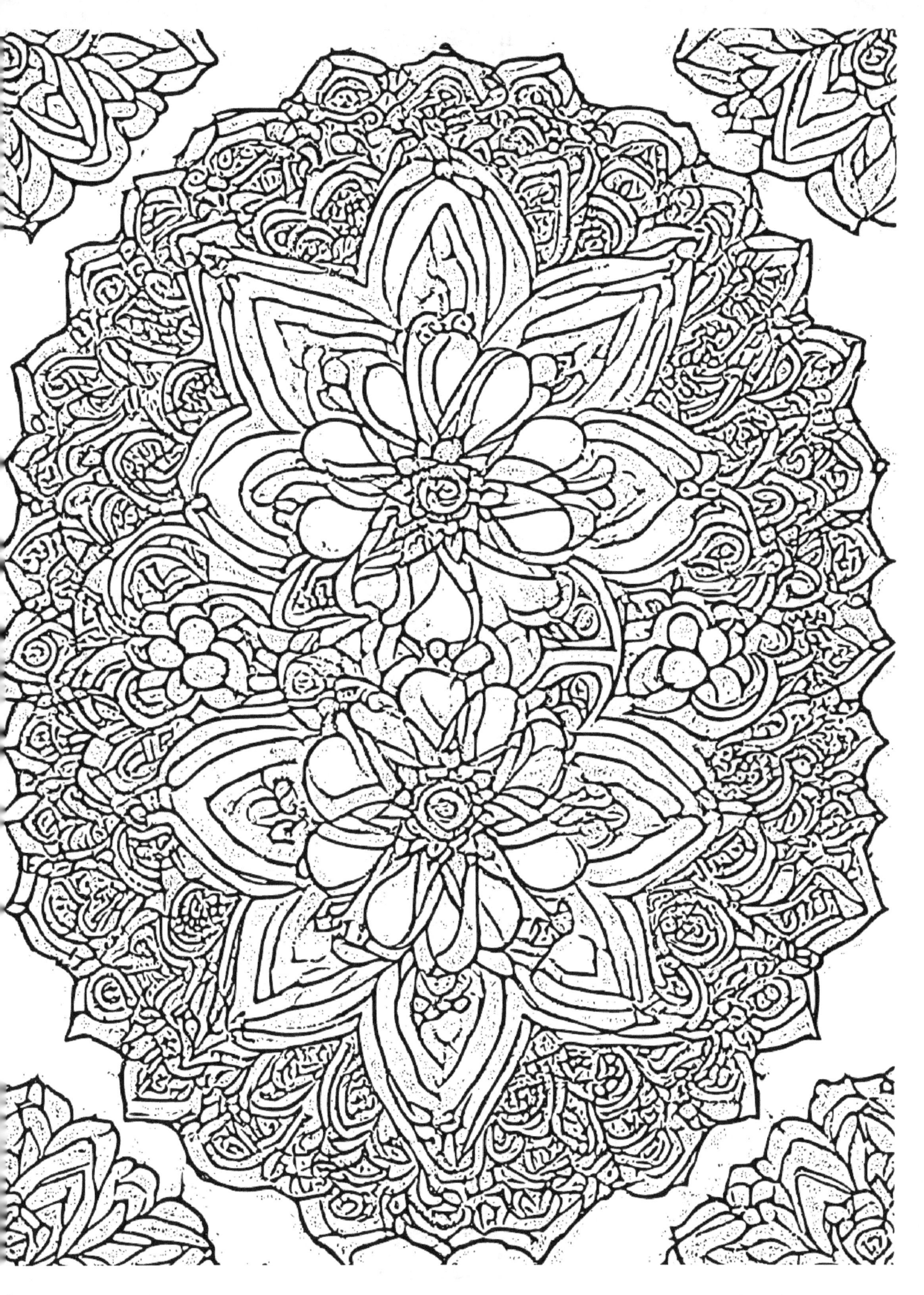

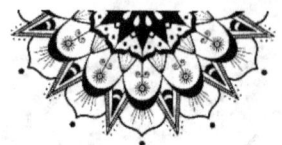

"The only true way to deal with our fears is to face them." - Bruce Lee

Notes

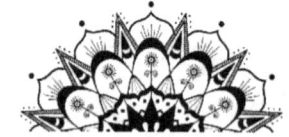

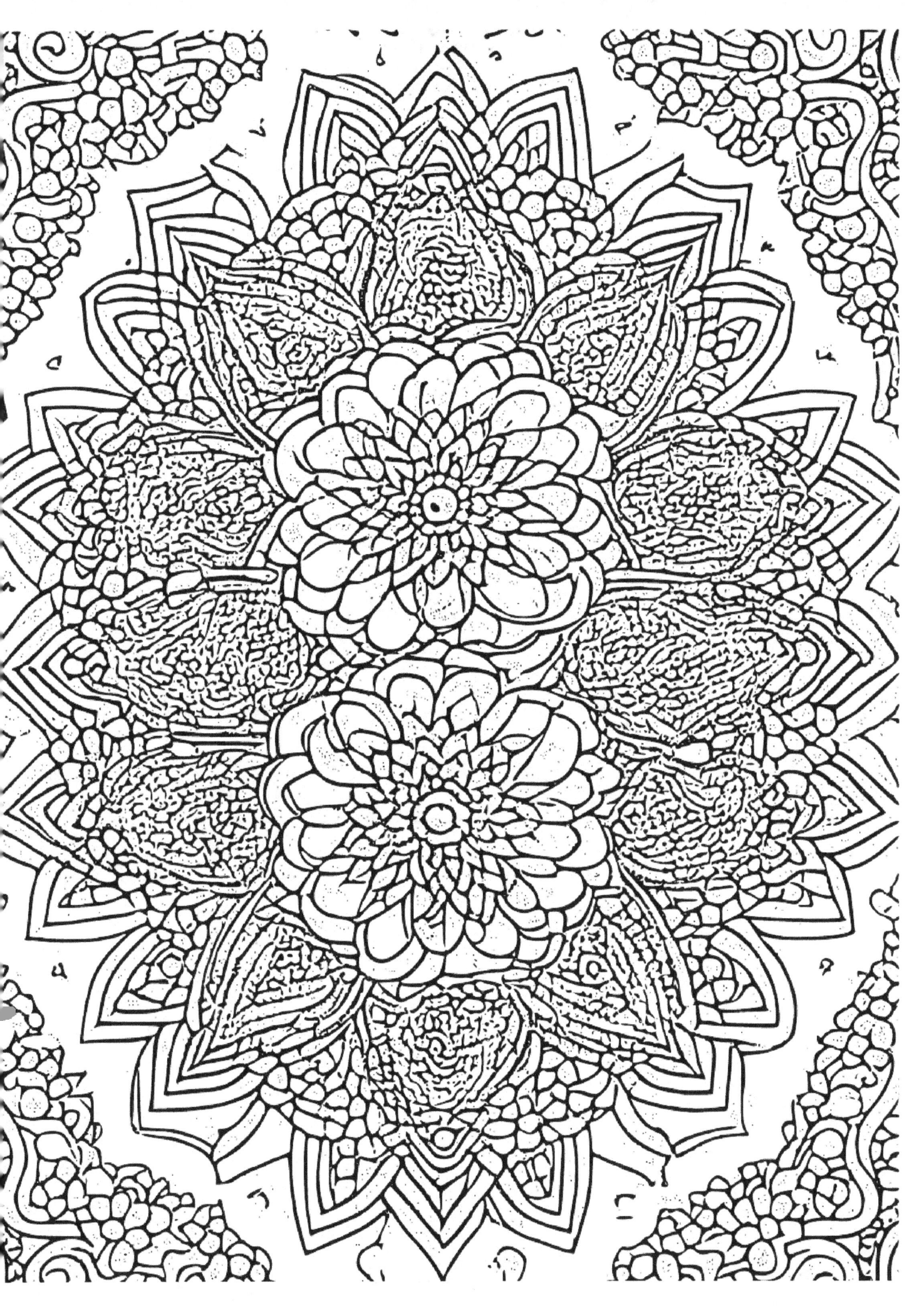

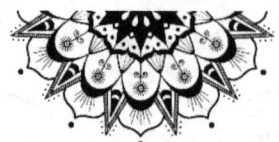

"Don't count the days, make the days count." - Muhammad Ali

Notes

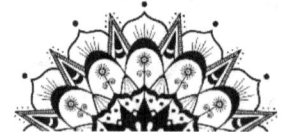

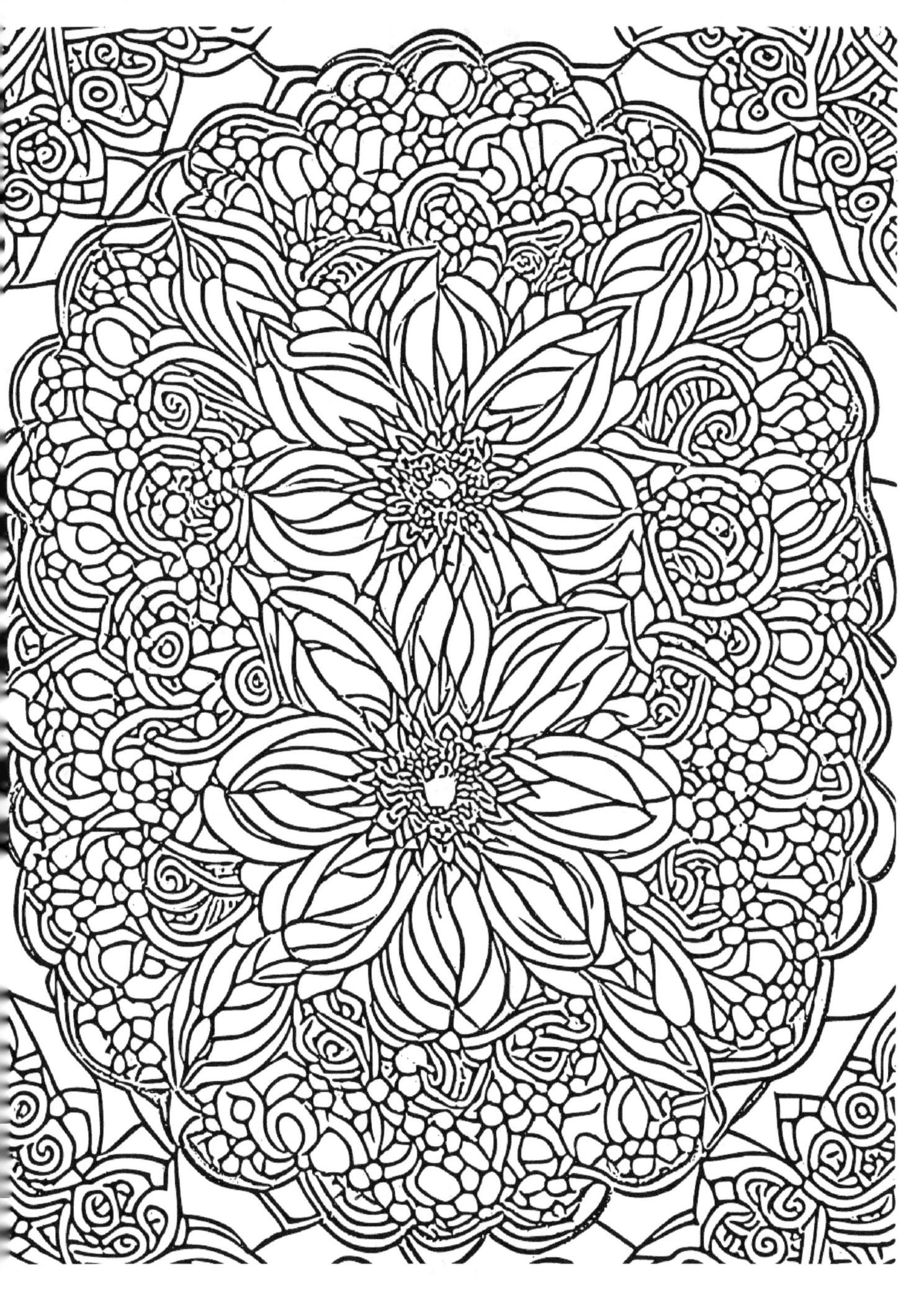

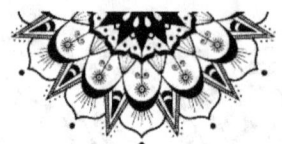

"Be yourself; everyone else is already taken." – Oscar Wilde

Notes

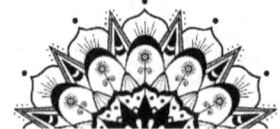

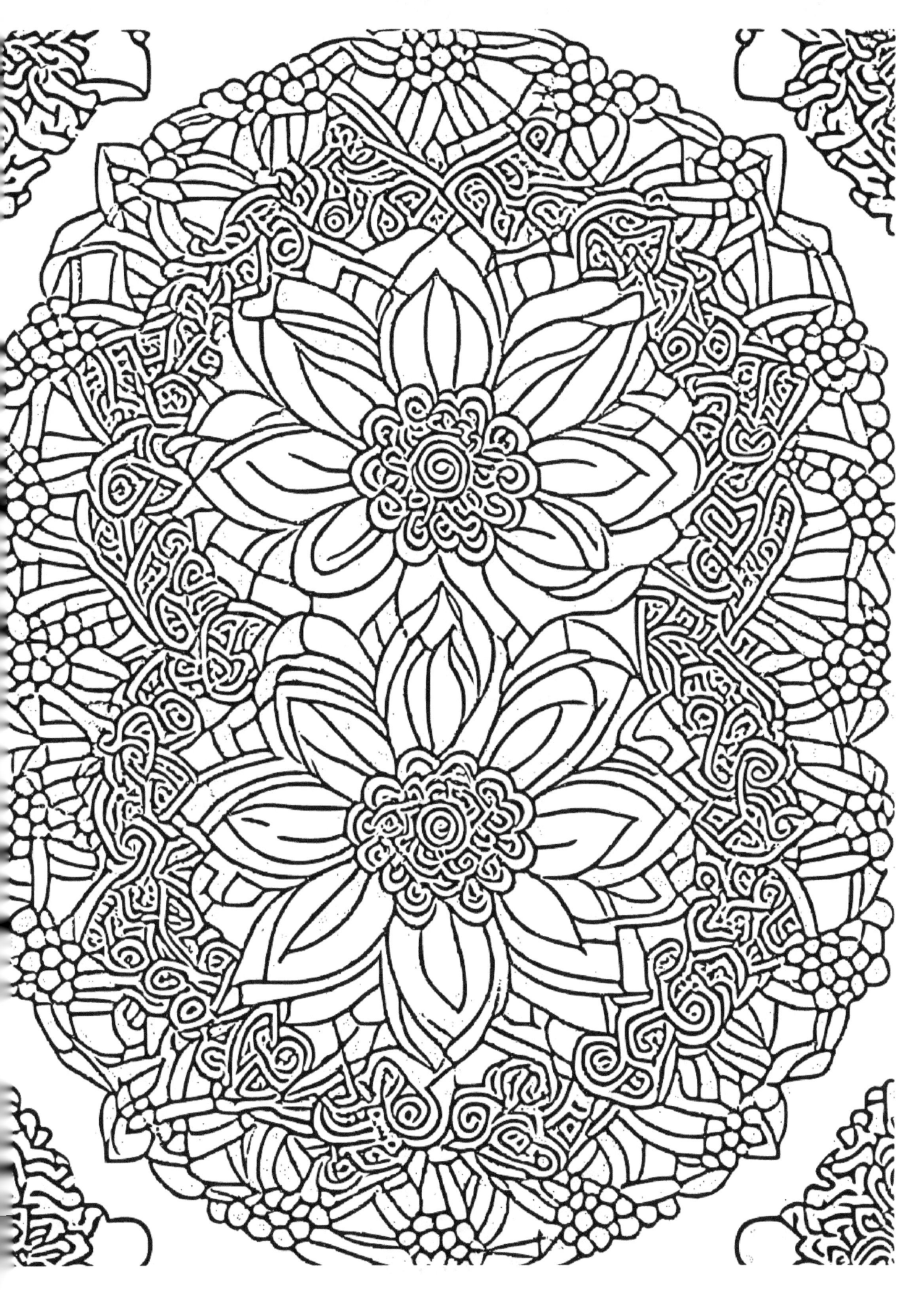

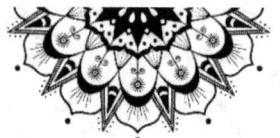

"The best revenge is massive success." - Frank Sinatra

Notes

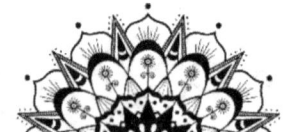

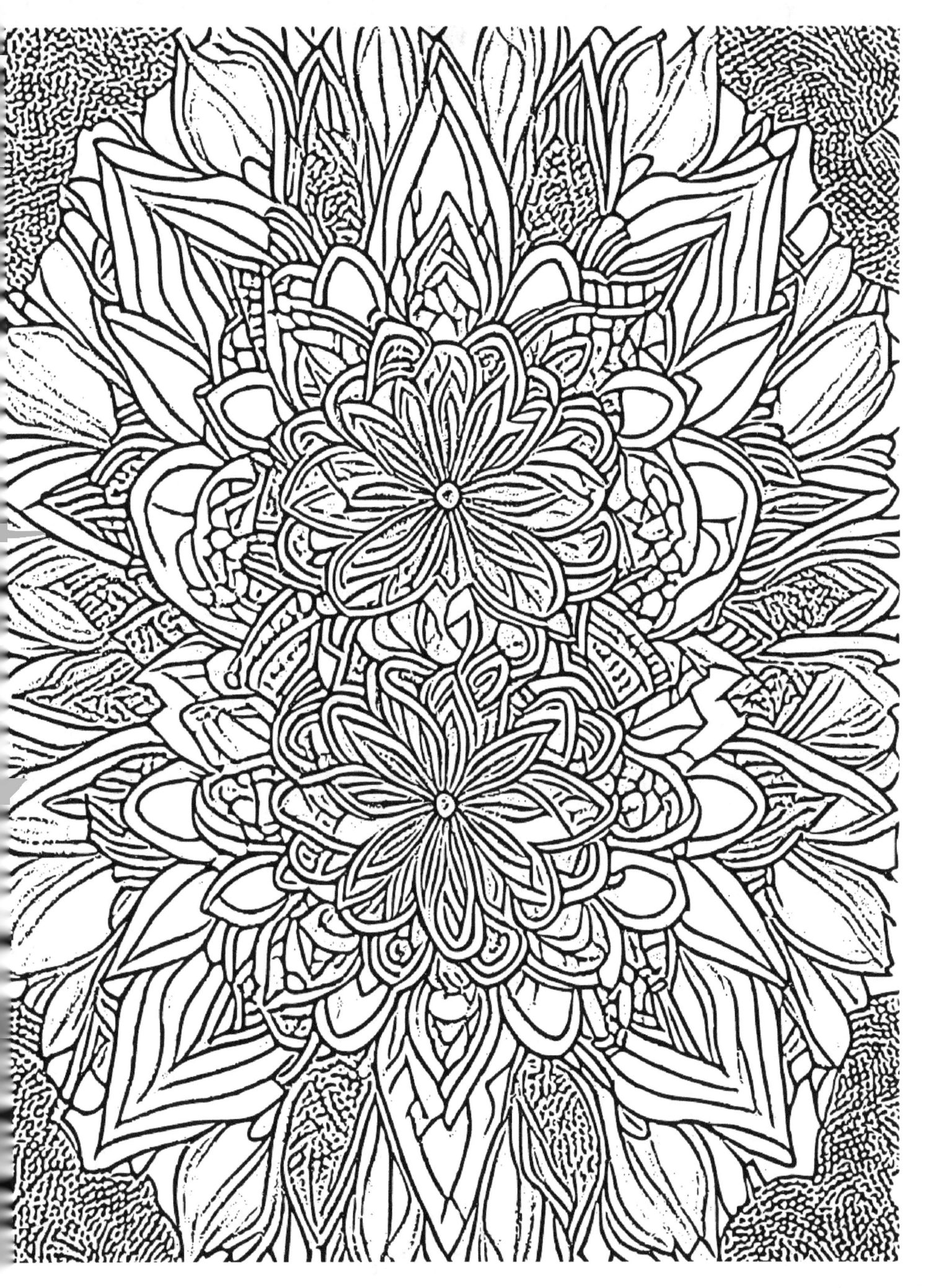

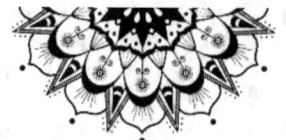

"Do what you can, with what you have, where you are." - Theodore Roosevelt

Notes

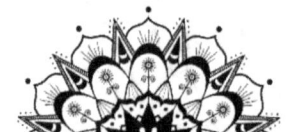

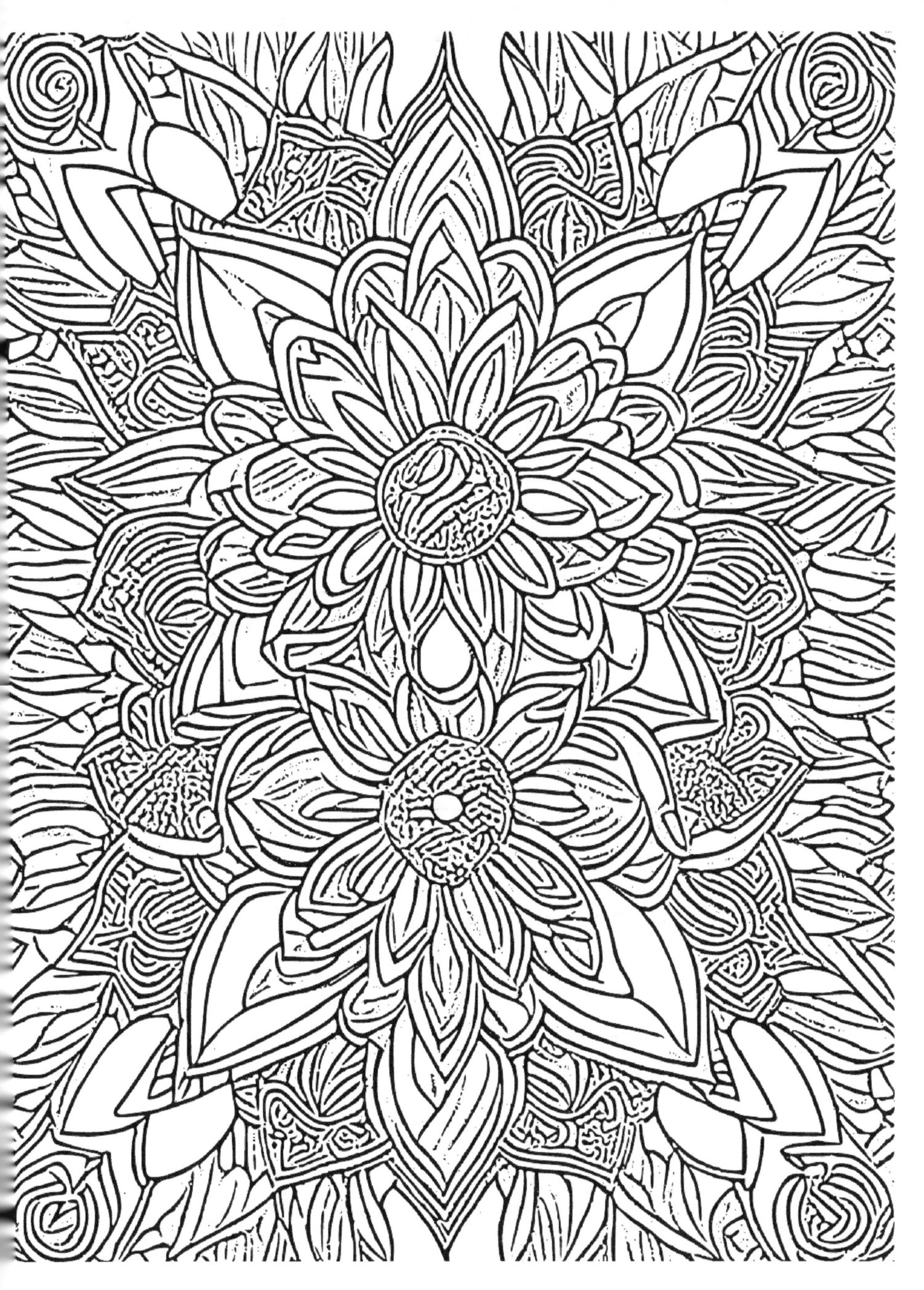

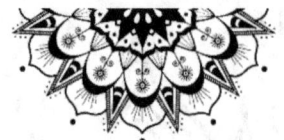

"Be the change that you wish to see in the world." - Mahatma Gandhi

Notes

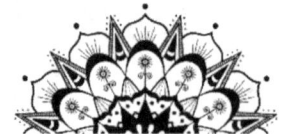

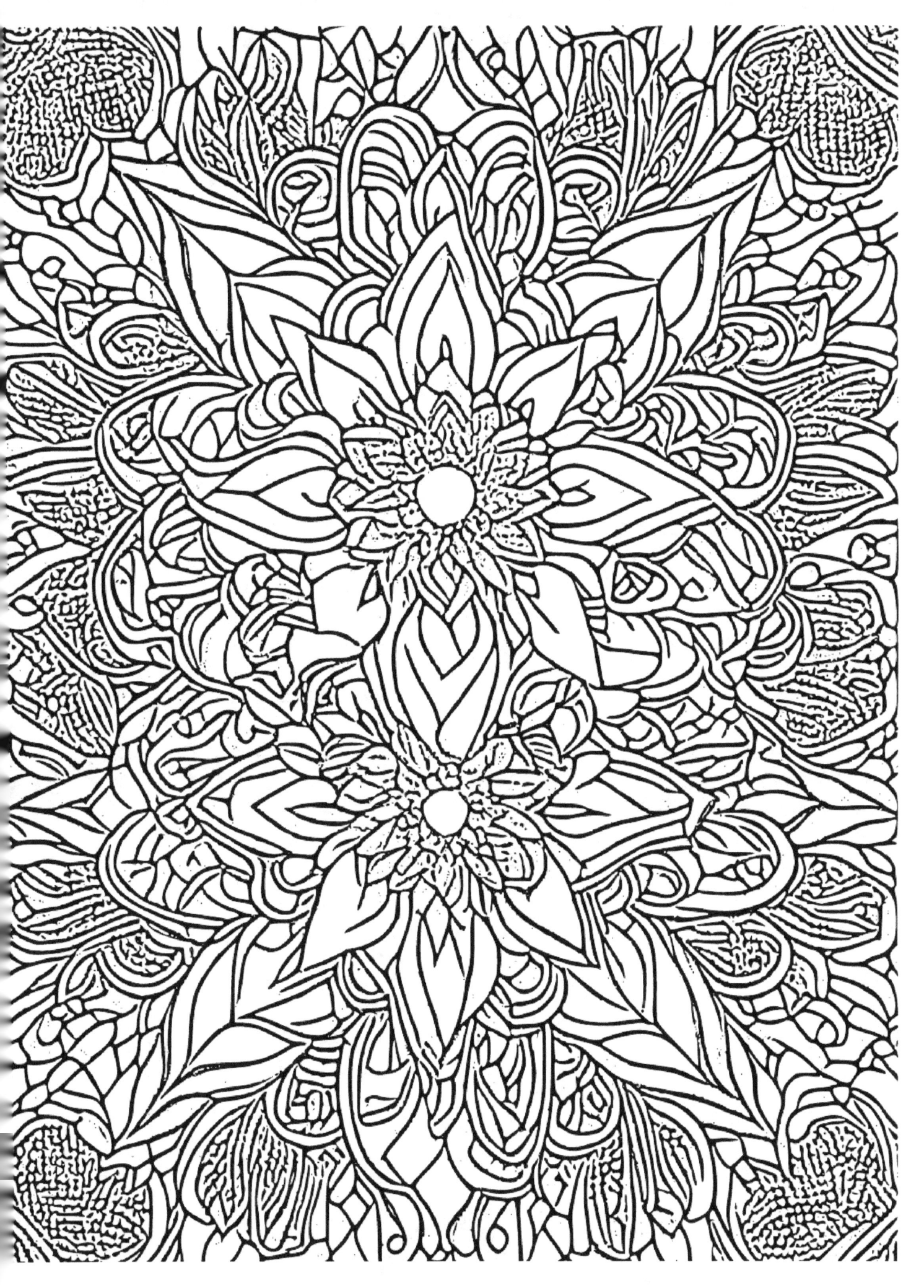

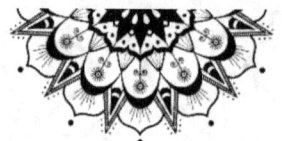

"Success is not in what you have, but who you are." - Bo Bennett

Notes

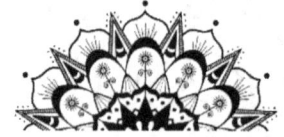

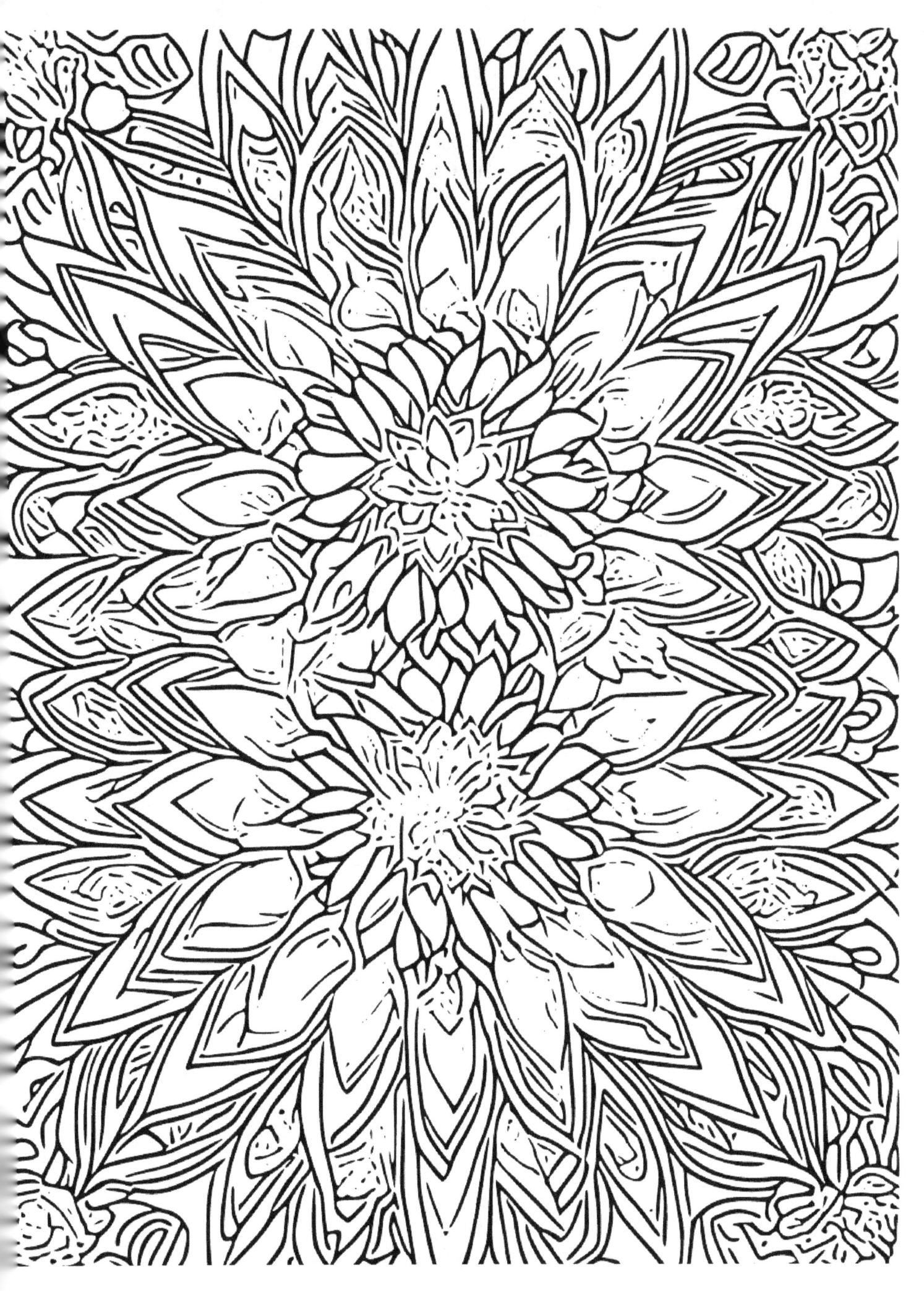

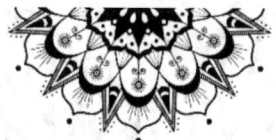

"The best time to plant a tree was 20 years ago. The second best time is now."
- Chinese Proverb

Notes

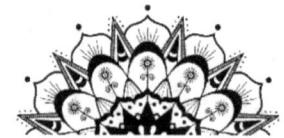

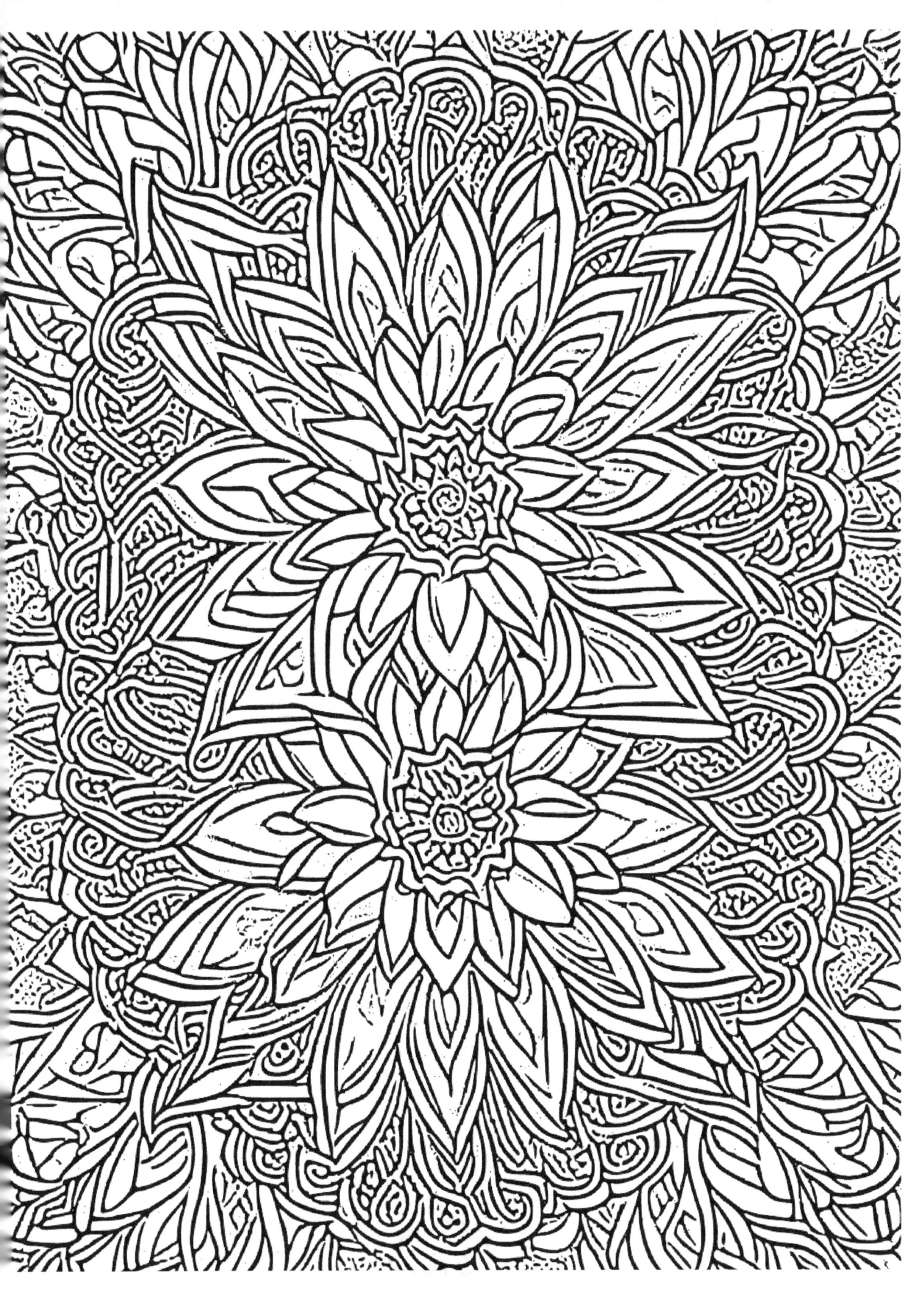

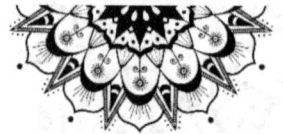

"The journey of a thousand miles begins with a single step." - Lao Tzu

Notes

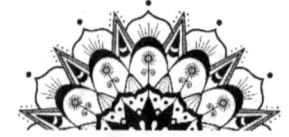

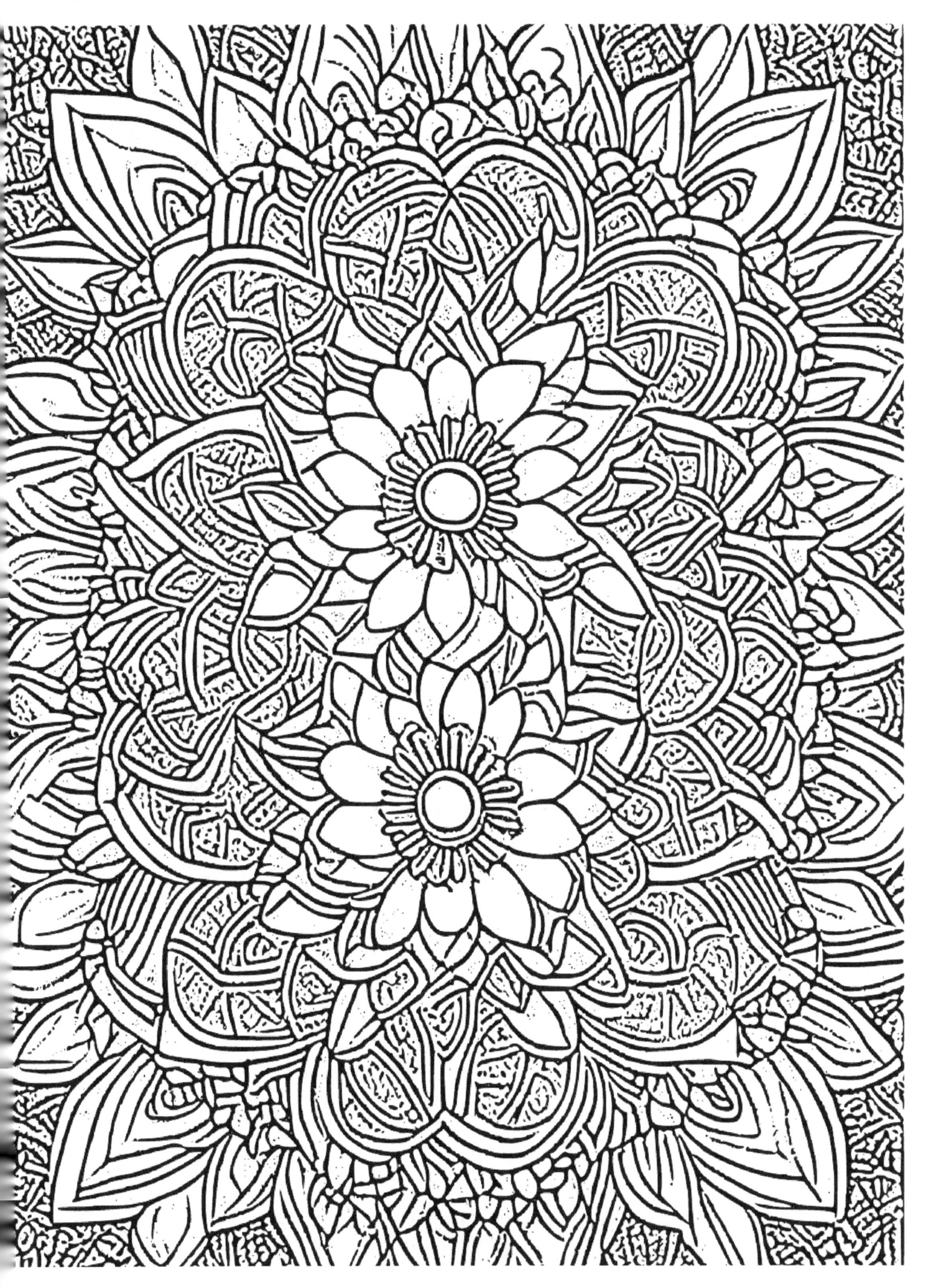

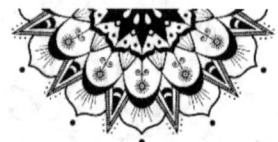

"Success is not the absence of failure; it's the persistence through failure." - Aisha Tyler

Notes

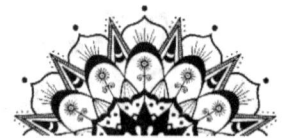

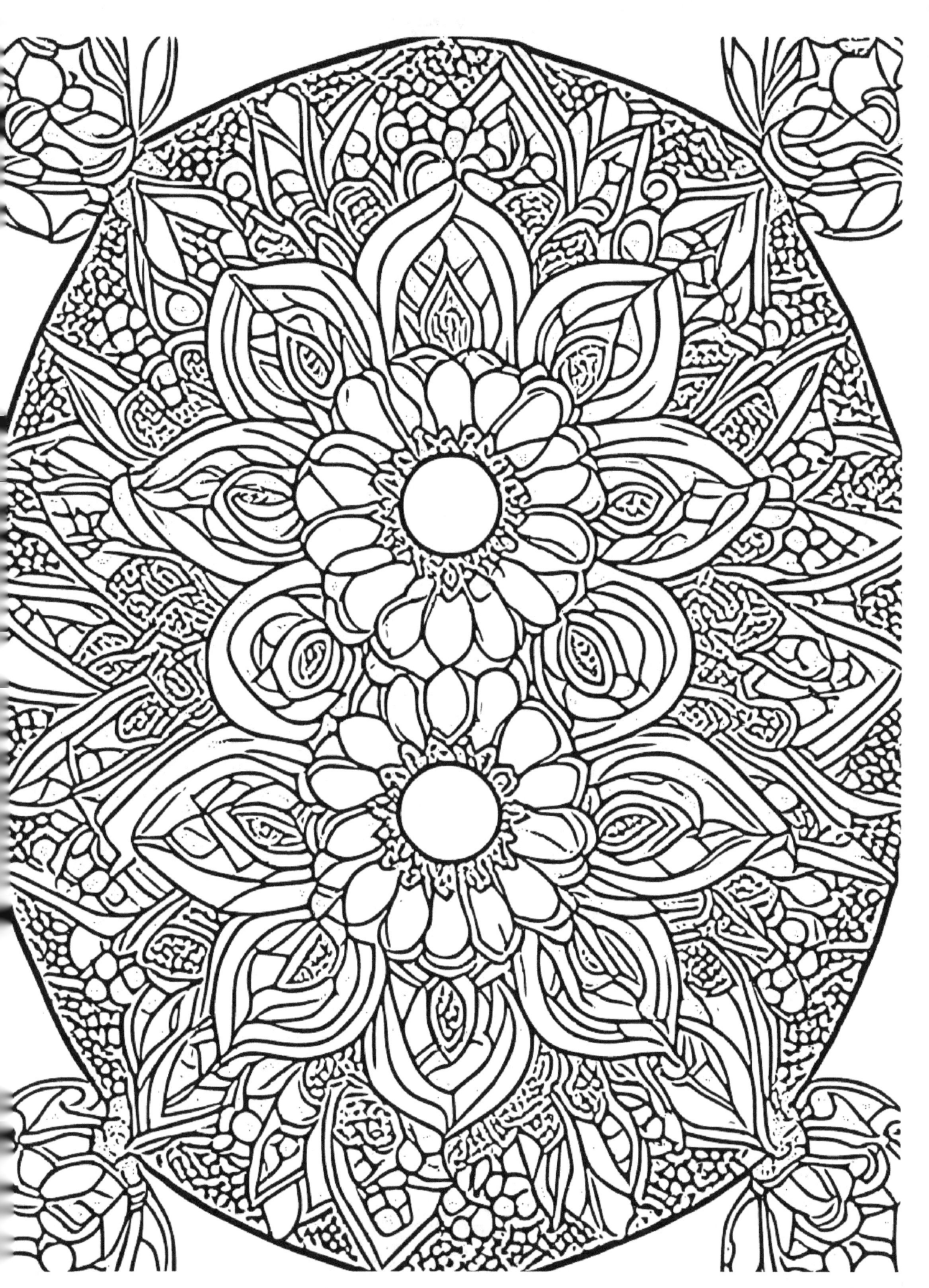

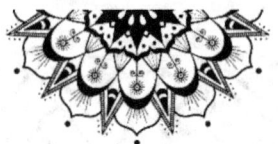

"The only thing standing between you and your goal is the story you keep telling yourself."
- Jordan Belfort

Notes

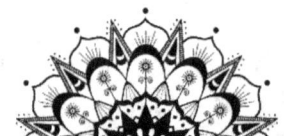

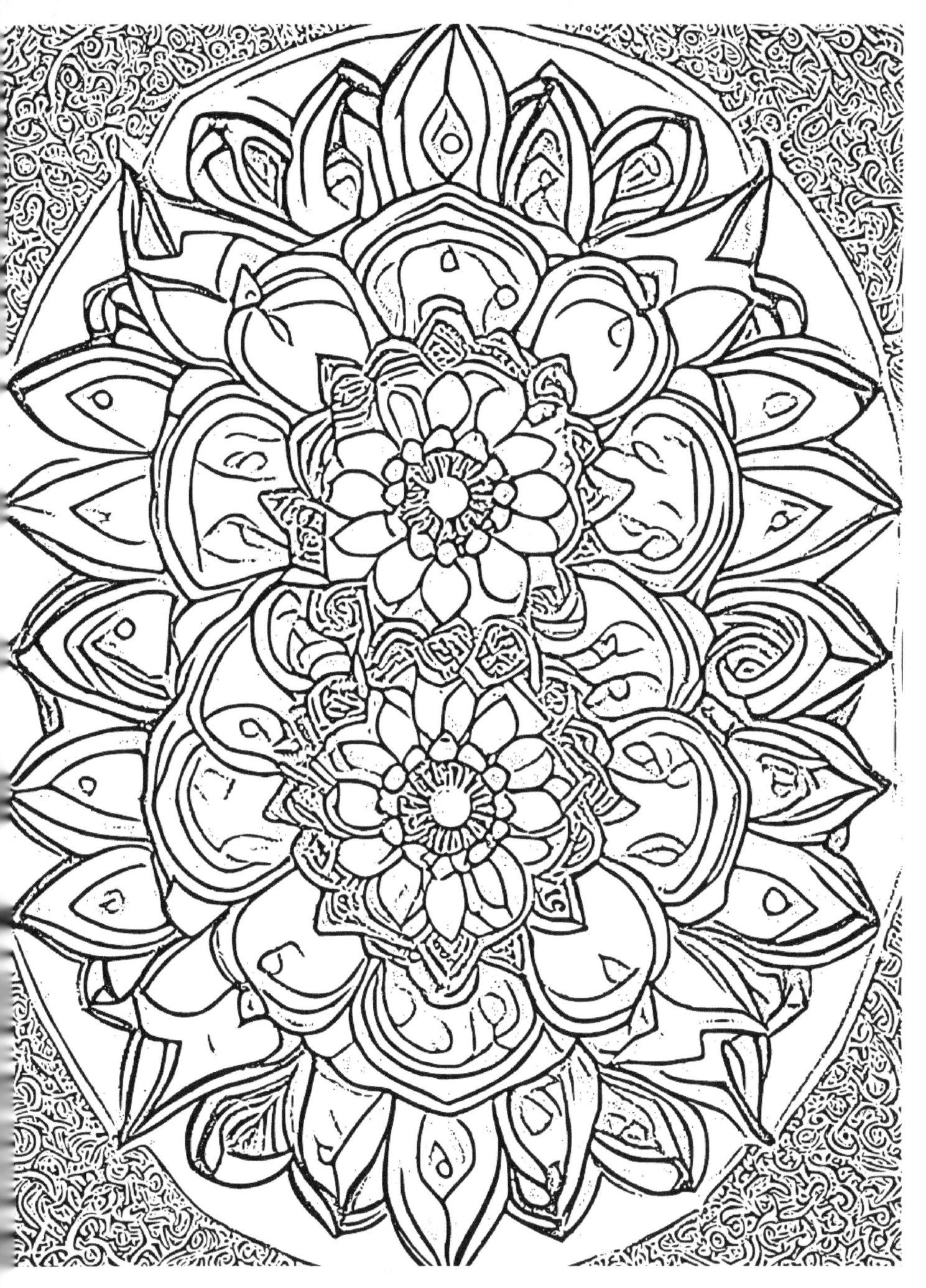

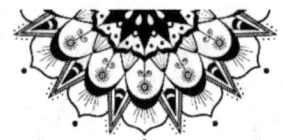

"The difference between a successful person and others is not a lack of strength, not a lack of knowledge, but rather a lack of will." - Vince Lombardi

Notes

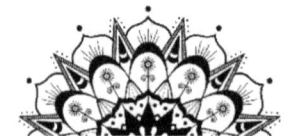

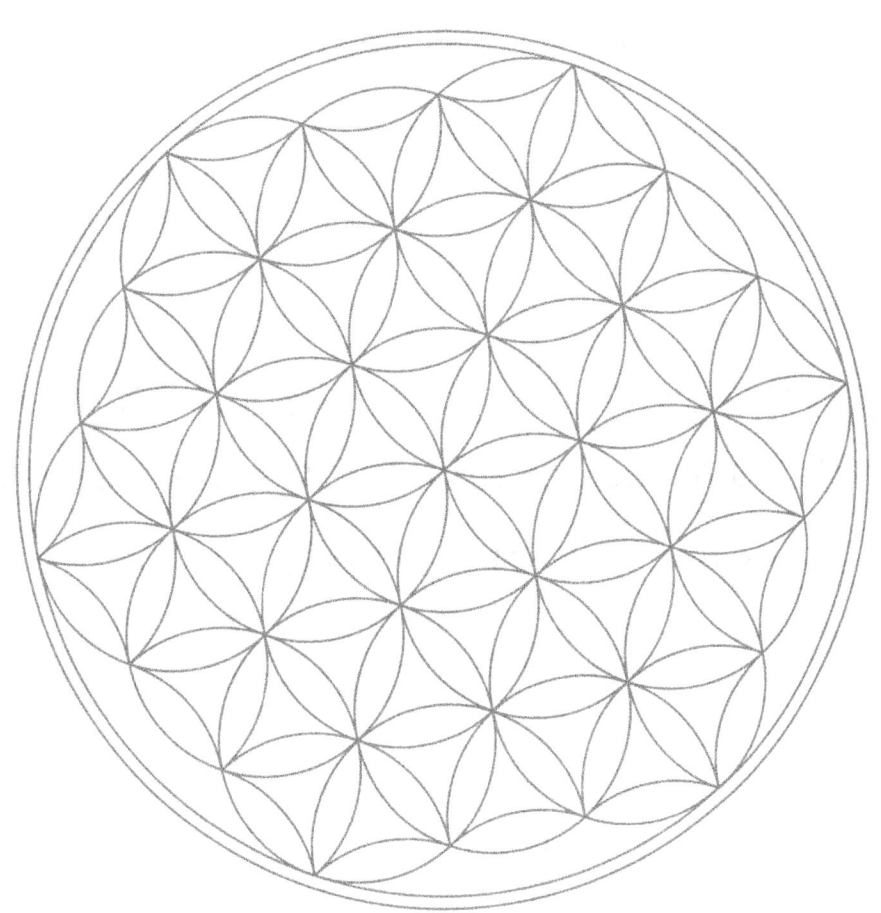